# VINTAGE CLOTHING

## 1880-1960

### Identification & Value Guide

by Maryanne Dolan

## 2nd Edition

ISBN 0-89689-063-5

*Distributed By*
**Gem Guides Book Co.**
3677 San Gabriel Parkway
Pico Rivera, Calif. 90660

# DEDICATION

**for my mother,**
**'A FASHION PLATE'**

# ACKNOWLEDGEMENTS

## WITH SPECIAL THANKS TO:

BUTTERICK FASHION MARKETING CO., New York

BUTTERFIELD & BUTTERFIELD, Auctioneers of San Francisco, Ca., particularly Douglas Sandberg and Patrick Sumner for their photographs of the Harrah's Museum auction.

Donna Charkowicz who owns the vintage clothing shop DRESSING UP in Oakland, California.

WILLIAM DOYLE GALLERIES of New York whose M. J. Flanagan supplied the photographs of the Ruth Gordon auction.

FOLKWEAR PATTERNS, San Rafael, California.

PETRA MARTIN for the photographs of her own splendid garments pictured in this book and for the use of the photos of the garments consigned to Butterfield's.

THE MUSEUM OF THE CITY OF NEW YORK for the photographs of the magnificent WORTH gowns.

SOUTHERN OREGON HISTORICAL SOCIETY, Jackson, Oregon.

Betty Williamson who caters to the special needs of the Vintage Car Collector.

**To my friends with gratitude for the loan of their treasures:**

Marlys Aboudara
Nan Almeida
Linda Baker
Virginia Cox
Beatrice Deasy
Pat & Henry Ewald
Clarice Hart
Betty Krueger
Pat LePage
Dorothy Malott
Thomas A. McGovern
Pearline Munson

**And to those who modeled:**

Lynn  Baer
April Brady
Donna Charkowicz
Virginia Cox
Amy Denebeim
Henry Ewald
Regina Gustason
Lauren Howard
Sheila Huth
Arlene Kozub
Kellene Kozub
Patty Long
Petra Martin
Pat Nagle
Evy Packer
Ann Thatcher
Pam Thatcher
Lynda Weir
Betty Williamson
John Williamson

# TABLE OF CONTENTS

# PREFACE

The world of vintage fashion has enlarged and deepened since the first edition of this book was published. More shops have opened, new collectors have been drawn to the field, and while more clothing has become available with the new knowledge, good pieces have become scarce. This is due to tremendous competition for the best of the past. Auctions now dedicated solely to vintage fashion have become almost commonplace and attract overflow crowds, more college programs have included courses in the history of fashion, more museums have added vintage clothing displays to their permanent exhibits, and collectors have become more sophisticated and selective.

Celebrity clothing has become a factor. The name of a famous owner coupled with that of a prestigious couturier is fast becoming an unbeatable combination and a collector goal. High fashion clothing with a designer label is an irresistible lure to those whose budgets are large.

There are several new stars in the garment galaxy; the Japanese kimono of the 1920's and 30's, eminently wearable with its sensuous materials and exotic designs; any garment boasting fine lace is a prime target; the cotton smocks, useful and inexpensive; shoes of all eras; the still undervalued furs, most particularly the sumptuous ermine; the off-beat handbags, hats and gloves of the 1940's and 50's continue to attract new collectors. The whole spectrum of the 1940's and 50's clothing is moving up rapidly in price as well as desirability. Shoe buckles have made an amazing impact on accessories collections and are now beginning to make rather spectacular price gains.

Competition for Victorian pieces has sharpened dramatically with the proliferation of the Horseless Carriage Clubs. As restoration of old automobiles becomes a bigger hobby, older clothing becomes a part of the process. The tours planned by classic car clubs require attendant appropriate period clothing and this field is becoming the specialized province of the dealer who caters to those who require a whole wardrobe in period. These buyers are highly selective, must match the age of their automobile and also require elaborate gowns to grace their formal affairs. It is a whole new aspect of vintage clothing collecting. Anyone who has ever seen one of these cavalcades of old vehicles cannot soon forget the accompanying stunning fashion show.

The almost incredible appeal of specialized societies such as the various Art Deco groups is having an enormous effect on the field. They, too, require clothing of a certain period to be worn to various functions, informal and formal. Anyone with an interest in vintage clothing and accessories should most certainly try for an invitation to one of their fashion shows or formal functions.

The lingerie of the 1930's through the 1950's is becoming increasingly sought after. It is often quite fancy and almost always dainty and thoroughly feminine. The slips are beautifully made to fit the figure in a flattering way and many are so pretty women claim to have worn them as formals. The strapless evening gown of the 1940's is in increasing demand and these dresses, which kept their wearers praying through hectic dances, are rapidly disappearing into collections, though in many cases their original owners still wear them and refuse to part with them.

Even a cursory glance at any high fashion magazine will indicate the extent to which the later clothing is valued. Contemporary designers borrow freely from the extravagant and flattering draping of the 40's dresses, from the back interest of the 30's gowns, and evening wear of heavy beading, that trademark of the 20's, is being shown everywhere on gowns imported into the United States. Three piece cotton play outfits are back in vogue; here and there a 60's mini-skirt is visible, and the almost fanatical interest in the fashions and accessories of the 1920's continues unabated. Supply can never keep up with demand so prices will continue to rise. The beaded dresses are literally coming out of the closet but are being snapped up as fast as they appear with prices spiraling upward.

The vagaries of fashion are numerous and unpredictable but certain truths are self-evident. The vintage clothing collector should choose the best of any and all periods to enhance a collection. Style outlasts any fad, the cut, the line, the trim of a garment tells its story. Good taste is always a good buy. The collector should exercise independent judgment so the collection will reflect personal preference.

Eventually there will be a sensible break in collecting periods – pre 1915 will be considered "old vintage" because of its very different feeling from what came after; the 1920's will probably always be categorized as a separate entity; the 1930's through the 1960's will be designated as "vintage." The advantage of later clothing for the collector is immediately apparent – it is abundant, it is reasonably priced, it is wearable and often it is quite beautiful. The truly magnificent old vintage clothing has reached the pinnacle of status but often calls for careful restoration so that future generations will be able to see its beauty and appreciate the skill involved in its making. Such restoration is the province of the very clever or the professional. Later clothing is still often found in remarkably good condition.

Recently I bought a 40's fedora for display. My college age son spied it, adopted it and wears it and loves it. Recently he left it behind in a movie theatre and when I called to determine if it was still there, a pleasant male voice assured me it was and he had been wearing it around the theatre. "That's a great hat," he said, "I love that hat."

That sums up the clothing collector, the older styles are often dashing and have verve and most of them have the same feeling as a much loved and lived-in older house, they have character and grace.

One of the really wonderful aspects of collecting clothing is that there is room for the collector to demonstrate the flair and style not always evident in everyday living, to live a fantasy life in a fairytale time of your own choosing. Above all, be true to your own style.

In 1928 THE TAILORED WOMAN, an elegant shop on Fifth Avenue, New York, trumpeted in a large advertisement which featured two tulle and chiffon designer dresses, unadorned by any glitter, WE DO NOT WASTE TIME ON BEADED DRESSES. "Everyone to his or her own taste," said that cagey old Roman, Horace; The Tailored Woman is long gone, but the beaded dress lives on.

*Maryanne Dolan*

138 Belle Avenue
Pleasant Hill, California 94523

# INTRODUCTION

Collecting vintage fashion becomes the art of the possible. The very material of which most clothing was made lends itself to destruction and the need to be in fashion which caused so many beautiful gowns to be discarded and neglected has left us with many gaps in our collection wardrobes.

Even the Smithsonian Institution has not been able to fully round out the Inaugural Gown collection of the First Ladies. Some of the gowns currently on exhibit were never worn to that First Ball, but are simply dresses of the period. So it is with the collector; if a primary sample of a period piece is not available, we must make do with a secondary example, or a dress or suit of the same period.

Indeed, so much High Fashion has been chronicled that a whole new wave of collectors dealing only with every day garments has surfaced, but most collectors today are seeking good samples of the great design periods, and this is a challenging, but rewarding task.

It can take you from specialized shops, to flea markets, to thrift shops, to second hand clothing stores and to friends and relatives with bulging closets or attics.

Competition in this field is becoming much keener and it behooves you to be pleasant to Aunt Minnie who may be harboring a Balenciaga somewhere.

Fortunately for us, many people refuse to discard anything and it is to them that we owe a large debt of gratitude for much of our older clothing. In most cases, since these people bothered to save it, they also took care of it.

Unless you are blessed with great skill at needlework, older clothing is often difficult to repair and restore with authenticity. The old taffeta, for example, had metallic thread to give it that rustle, but it also caused it to rot away, so you seldom see an old taffeta dress in mint condition and it is almost impossible to repair. The best advice is to take your restorable, valuable clothing to an expert. In many cases museums dealing with vintage clothing offer such services, and if they do not, can probably recommend a specialist in this narrow field.

If the price is right, and the damage slight or not too obvious, buy the piece and then think about restoration. "If the Price is Right" should be emblazoned above every clothing collector's closet these days when the large auction houses are organizing special auctions of high fashion vintage clothing and selling it for high sums.

The average collector today should keep in mind the fragility of his or her collectible, the competition for this clothing, the escalating prices and need for less procrastination. Someone, if it's a fair price, will buy that gorgeous gown before you can say Schiaparelli.

Collectors should look for rare pieces in good condition, the choice Victorian pieces or the 20's dresses that are beaded and in excellent condition. Remember that all of the 1920's dresses were not hand beaded but that does not seem to be of tremendous import to collectors; what should rank very high on your list of requirements for any garment is the basic design, the material, and the way the garment was made.

The vintage clothing collector has chosen a field which excels in great beauty and interest; it deals with design, with fabrics of types sometimes rare and expensive, with braids and lace, and feathers and beads; it makes a definitive comment on history and what people did and what they wore for their work and leisure. It is often a collectible of remarkable elegance and above all it is a reflection on the collector, for anyone who chooses this field must be a person of awareness and taste.

The collection should speak for itself, through you, and the statement it makes says as much about you, the collector, as it does about the person who originally wore it.

# CHAPTER ONE
# 1880-1900

The primary collecting area in the field of Vintage Fashion occurs after 1880, beyond that we are dealing with the very rare and expensive garment which has now become the province of the museums and affluent collector. True, the occasional 1860's or 1870's dress or hat or bonnet will turn up to lend excitement to the chase, but the practical collector will choose a later period which lends itself to easier acquisitions.

By the 1880's the bustle using a wire support was back in style and the feet were visible below a slightly shortened skirt. That seemed to be as far as women were allowed to display any part of the anatomy, and unfortunately for females of the 1880's and 1890's, fashion dictated such a plethora of clothing for ordinary wear that one wag was inspired to say that planning the Parthenon probably took less time than his wife's daily toilette.

Too true, imagine yourself day after dreary day preparing to go outdoors; the corset, the drawers, the bodice, petticoats and more petticoats, and often so many buttons down the back help was needed to dress.

The Victorians loved clutter in all things, their houses were shrines to that particular god, knick-knacks everywhere, not an inch of shelf or table space left unoccupied. It seems fitting then that the women who dictated these arrangements also cluttered their persons. Not only was the clothing complicated and overdone, but the coiffure was also a tribute to the complex, calling for front curls and whatever one favored in back. False hairpieces were popular, some made from the combings of the Victorian woman herself; braids, or plaits as they were referred to, chignons, loops; the more elaborate the better.

Ribbons and feathers and flowers were much in evidence on the bonnets which were so varied and eyecatching they are greatly prized today by collectors.

The 1880's bustle differed from that of the 1870's, but the whole effect in the first years of the 1880's was one of rigidity and stiffness, which ironically or not, complemented the Victorian attitudes.

Dresses were heavier, and skirts began to increase in size.

Men's clothing was somber and conformed to the new image of the successful industrialist. Single-breasted jackets and straightline, longish, frock coats, worn with straight trousers without a crease, prevailed. The clothing atmosphere was one of inflexibility and propriety, and in female fashion, not always particularly pretty.

From her well-shod feet to her beribboned bonnet, the lady of the 1880's was as encased by her clothing as she was by the conventions of the day. For the collector of the fashions of those years, the clothes are highly desirable, but not readily available. It is wise to comb attics and old trunks, especially if your family has been an acquisitive one, for it is usually in this way that the collector has the best chance of coming upon these treasures.

To us, in 1987, they seem as other-worldly as the 17th century laces and satins must have seemed to the Victorian, they were uncomfortable, restrictive and not overly flattering, but they appeal to our fantasy lives, says one dealer, and the best of the clothing represents good workmanship and often good design in what was an era of peace and plenty and sturdy family life. The garments are part of that nostalgia, they have an aura of stability.

One of the loveliest of all collectibles springs from the 1880's – the shawl. Shawls are still worn today, they are useful and graceful, but the biggest thing in shawls for the Victorian lady was Paisley. The colorful, swirled patterns of abstract, curved shapes are felt to have derived from the patterns of Persian rugs and the name itself from Paisley, Scotland. It was far and away the most popular type, although these shoulder coverings came in a great variety of sizes and materials. If the budget does not lend itself to the dresses and suits of the Victorian age, try shawls, with their heavy fringes and bright colors they can be used in a variety of ways, even as wall hangings. They are still fairly easy to find although serious collectors have long been seeking them and there are now many museum displays which feature them. They are without doubt one of the genuine markers of the age and some collectors use them as a backdrop to a clothing collection.

As the 1880's gave way to the 1890's the silhouette began to show signs of adapting to the emerging woman. Paris still had a firm hold on the fashion world, although women were showing signs of making their own decisions about what they wanted to wear and how they wanted to look. Men, too, began to feel stifled, but in spite of the tendencies of a group called the 'Aesthes' with their fancy vests and velvet jackets and their preference for color, the basic shape did not change much. The accessories were engaging though, and lent an air of the rakish to the men of fashion – the cane, the elegant watches, the fobs, the hats – all of which are diligently hunted today.

By the 1890's the shape of the female gown had become softer and looser. The sleeve, always a good indicator of the period of early clothing, now showed some fullness at the top and by the late 1890's had expanded considerably.

But the biggest revolution in clothing was caused by the wheel. Or two wheels – the bicycle. It became an absolute passion and while we may find it hard to conceive of cycling with large, veiled hats and full length skirts and often rather formal looking blouses, think of the men doomed to hats and coats and ties while they pedaled. Still, after being repressed for so long the bicycle must have seemed like the ultimate in freedom. Where the wealthy had their horses and carriages, now everyone could indulge the craving for mobility at little expense. Naturally, not everybody was content to ride as if dressed for a party, so it was only natural that clothing modification would follow.

The bustle disappeared. Knickerbockers became the number one item on the fashion agenda. Both men and women wore them and the difference was the women's were much fuller. Hats were still worn, and jackets but men adopted the cap too, and younger boys really admired this casual style. The whole 1890's world was cycling, everybody was on the move. Skirts eventually replaced the knickers for women and they were full and easy to manage. Women's Lib wasn't even a gleam in the female eye, but the clothes were telling us something.

The 1890's female preferred such materials as gauze, and the old time silk warp challies, black taffeta was still popular and cashmeres and organdies and a new canvas cloth in fancy weave called 'Mouline natte' flourished. Transparent fabrics such as grenadine, mousseline de soie, chiffon and the small standing collar became part of the fashion scene, especially for Spring. Flowers, vines, scrolls, trimmings of blossoms and leaves covering these light fabrics lent a feminine look.

"Eighteen ninety eight," boasted a woman's magazine, "was a time to buy stripes, and all cord effects are safe for the coming season. Tucks will run crosswise on waist and sleeves and around the skirt, while braids, insertions, ruffles and all decoration will follow in the same path." Ruffles did indeed flourish in every possible width on that year's Summer fashions to such an extent that they often overshadowed the gown itself. Collectors today who find a gown of that era in less than repairable condition, tend to strip it of its laces and ruffles for possible use elsewhere. Do not overlook the possibilities of a gown in very poor condition which may cost too much to have refurbished. If the price is right, its trimmings, even to the buttons, can be useful as a collectible.

The seven gore skirt was in vogue and if you have the good fortune to own or to be able to examine a skirt made in this way, it is clearly a clever way of fitting the garment smoothly across the front and hips and giving it a graceful fullness at the back. For those interested, not only in the clothing of the day, but the way it was made, this type skirt has a dip in the back which is given more by the bias back seam than by the added length at the bottom. In certain materials, such as wool, this was a rather flowing cut and flattering. Wool was a favorite for clothing of this period and much of it is still in surprisingly good condition.

The late 1800's allowed for almost any color, any material or shape in women's dresses, although black dominated colorwise and the foulard again was gaining favor. Although the name 'foulard' is used again and again in fashion writings of the day and we can assume that it communicated itself immediately to the women who read the writings, it is not something most of us hear much about today. It encompasses several fabrics, it is a lightweight twill or plain woven silk, or silk and cotton, and it usually has a small printed design. The fabrics used in the more expensive gowns of the late 1800's were made over using the original material. Sometimes this was done more than once so if the needlewoman was skilled, we often cannot date a dress accurately.

White crepe de chine sounds seductive now, and indeed it was meant to be then. Dresses made of this often have fascinating trim, narrow lace ruffles, or deep ruffles edged with lace. This silk crepe makes any garment we find today expensive, but it is usually quite beautiful.

Sleeves of that day were distinctive and more than anything else give the garments the look we most associate with the period. They were generally long and trimmed at the top, cuffs or edgings were usually seen at the wrist. By the turn of the century, the ideal, unrealistic goal in waistlines was 19 inches. There were cases of ruined health by women seeking the impossible.

The designers were handling fashion as if it were great art. The upper sleeves were very large and full and balanced horizontally with the hem of the skirt, but the eye was drawn inevitably to the tiny waist. It is an exercise in proportion and these designers did their work so well that it is the silhouette which comes to mind, rather than individual garments when we think of the late 1890's.

It would probably send the Victorian lady into a state of shock if she realized that collectors of 1987 are madly seeking her underwear. Back to Basics might well designate collections of undergarments of the 1880-1890 period. There is more underclothing available to the collector than would seem possible, probably because women wore so much of it, a goodly quantity of it has survived. The underthings were cleverly engineered to nip in or add on, tighten or disguise. Nobody's perfect, so there was plenty of it made, and plenty of it now to choose from.

The corset is legendary and one wonders today how women were ever coerced into wearing them. They were linen covered, shaped with whalebone or steel. The whalebone lent flexibility to the corset and was not so heavy as the steel, but in either case the corset could be considered a dangerous garment. Smelling salts were big sellers and it probably had to do with the tight corset.

Today we look on these as high collectibles, particularly from a museum standpoint. Several major museums have mounted showings of the corset, and in this kind of viewing they do have a certain fascination, and in the abstract, were often beautifully made; from a practical standpoint women of the 1980's should give daily thanks for their liberation from this undergarment.

It's questionable who suffered more from this fashion – the Right Whale which almost became extinct or the woman who wore the corset. It is not rare to find these, especially those with the steel ribs. Some have been found in the original boxes in pristine condition. Even then there were women who refused to conform or was it just faint heart?

Drawers, which are simply a takeoff of longish underpants are a wonderful addition to a collection. They are charming in an innocent, long-ago sense. They were meant to cover the 'limbs' and were popular for a very long time. Most of the surviving drawers, and indeed a surprising number have survived, are elegantly ribboned and trimmed with lace, but even the simpler ones are real conversation pieces. These undergarments, unless unusually elaborate, are more easily cared for than the dresses or suits since their basic material was cotton or muslin. It is a fast growing segment of the vintage clothing field.

Another interesting and overlooked collectible is the apron.

For everyday household chores, the apron was in full swing in the 1880-1890 period. The lifestyle of women still dictated their almost total commitment to the home and although women were beginning to emerge into the workforce, house and hearth was still the lodestar of their existence. So aprons were not only necessary, but fashion magazines of the day spent much space discussing this covering. Nowadays the apron is an anachorism except the frothy little concoctions we tend to don during the holiday season, or the barbecue aprons sported by men who feel more in the cordon bleu spirit when the voluminous garment is covering them.

The 1890's lifestyle dictated the use of the apron.

Afternoon tea was an ordinary aspect of life and demanded a covering for the dress of the young lady who did the pouring. These were fancy, net or lace, made in any way the owner chose, but reaching to the knee and made rather narrow. Some exist of Valenciennes or Brussels lace with very elaborate trimmings. There were fancywork aprons for needlework – embroidery was popular because even at leisure hands should not be idle – and, of course, the ordinary work-a-day aprons. These were generally about two-thirds length and were made of lawn, nainsook or dimity, but were also trimmed to relieve the plainness. These materials could be laundered fairly easily, a necessity for the working apron.

The apron wardrobe was large and diverse. There were sewing aprons, servants aprons, nurses aprons, the aprons artists wore, kitchen aprons, children's aprons and most interesting of all as a social commentary, the aprons worn by the new young women who were beginning to take jobs. The worked behind the counters or were moving into offices as 'typewriters'. To cover their clothing they wore simple aprons of black cambric or sateen which was made of 2 lengths of material hemmed together to a belt and either buttoned in back or tied with long, black strings. These reached the bottom of the skirt and had at least one pocket. These intrepid women also wore cuffs which often matched the apron.

Very few vintage clothing collectors have, as yet, focused on this area, but it is interesting and often delightful. It is challenging too, but a good, representative collection of aprons could be made from the 1880's to the 1980's, and it is yet an inexpensive way to collect.

Aprons are beginning to appear in the shops, many reminiscent of a very different lifestyle. Not so glamorous as the designer clothing, or even the less costly pretty day dresses, aprons are a relatively untapped field, different, and because they are available and reasonably priced, rewarding.

These lesser collectibles within the large category of Vintage Fashion can be formed into deep and valuable categories of objects, certain to appreciate in value as well as interest, so always keep the accessories in mind when you buy older clothing.

Accessories were abundant in pre-1900 America. There was such a myriad of things with which to complement an ensemble that the mind boggles. Fashion maintained that these little trifles could be added to suit one's individual taste, and so the belts were often jeweled with precious gems or imitation stones, but silver and turquoise were favorites for the shirtwaist costume, emeralds and gold for blouses of velvet. Gold filigree belts were in vogue and the waist fell to the hemline and all manner of clever sash arrangements, as well as chiffon or lace or silk neck arrangements which tied under the chin were worn. Such short tie arrangements are still seen.

Veils were considered in fashion although ladies were warned that if the veils were dotted and "if the dots are too close, they will throw shadows on the face, but if scattered widely will have a flattering effect." Another typical fashion which seems forever etched in our consciousness is the empire scarf which was over 2 yards long and was meant to be fastened about the brim of the hat, crossed at the back and brought around and knotted on the left shoulder. A very romantic picture this, but not many seem to have survived. A favorite for this kind of scarf was Palin Brussels net so we are sometimes deceived into looking for chiffon and gauze and bypass the net.

Somewhat larger fans, feather ones or net or silk or gauze; suede gloves and suede dancing slippers were all the crack, and are all to be ardently embraced when discovered. Fan collectors have long been active, but gloves are still, for the most part, lying in piles in out of the way boxes in shops, and they are still in the bargain category.

The freedoms which were coming were certainly manifesting themselves in fashion. Whereas black stockings had been de rigueur, now plaids or stripes, even embroidered effects replaced the rather elegant black, and polka dot hosiery was said to be a big seller. For the collector, finding a pair of hose of this era is a tremendous find. Usually when they are available, it is hosiery which had never been worn and simply laid away. Just as today the stockings were not much considered, and having served their purpose were discarded. Probably it is best to consider the hosiery a bonus to your clothing collection, never stop looking for it, but don't expect to find it too often. Recently I saw a pair of Victorian spats for $30. Condition was excellent and before I could say, "I'll take them," they were bought by someone more decisive than I. Anything to do with the years 1880-1890 will sell because it can no longer be treated lightly, it is definitely museum bait.

Combs, too, have always had their devotees. The comb suited the pompadour hair style very well and were ornate and bejeweled and bedazzled the onlooker with multi-colored stones. There are many quite large and lovely comb collections already in existence, and not every clothing collector includes examples, although a comb lends authenticity to the dress. In collecting garments it is well to remember their context and if possible, to add a few of the accessories typical of their period. Even the august Smithsonian Institution has begun to equate the First Ladies gown collection with the rooms and artifacts of their times. If a collector strives to add some good quality items which tend to be silent pointers to the era it can only add interest and piquancy.

Children's fashions have always had appeal. Probably during the 1880-1890 period it was Kate Greenaway who most influenced their design. The popular artist of the 1890's depicted children dressed much as they would have been a century earlier, in the 1880's the Little Lord Fauntleroy look was introduced by the illustrations in the novel, the black velvet suit with a lace collar and plumed hat. A television rerun of the old film recently held a group of young people in thrall, so who knows what the future holds for little boys clothes.

Children seem always to have had more freedom in their clothing than the adults of the same time, and of course the infants were dressed in long dresses regardless of their sex. One of the great guides in this field are the old catalogues if precise dating is desired, but in the case of children, clothes were often handed down and may have been worn years after their purchase. From about the end of World War I, the whole world wanted to look young, and both children and adults wore much the same styles. Children's clothing is rather specialized, it tends to be expensive when the garment is old and attractive, and not all dealers handle it. It certainly lends authenticity to a collection and should be actively sought out if your aim is for all clothing of a certain period. People who love this type of apparel could not choose a more endearing type, if you do buy the dresses and suits worn by youngsters, search assiduously for the shoes, they are very special.

As in any collecting field, the fashion collector should be aware of developing trends. Today the Victorian wedding gown is one of the most desired of all garments. Young women are buying them to use just as they were originally intended and this fits into the general passion we all have for nostalgia.

Actually, the white gown and veil with orange blossoms was a Victorian invention. The gown was not meant to be put away after the wedding. It was to be used as a formal dress, or evening dress. My great grandmother's wedding dress of the 1880's shows much wear indicating it did double duty long after the wedding itself, it was not put away after the ceremony in tissue and into the cedar chest. It had never been intended for that fate.

The Victorian wedding dress can be magnificent, the best of them are overwhelming. The long train, the sleeves, full at the top, the luxurious fabric and the veil, often of precious lace crowned with either artificial or real orange blossoms. Not all of them had the large sleeves or the train and some are very simple, which proves once again that accurate dating in clothing is sometimes difficult.

While details have significance for the collector, it is more important to try to date by period divisions as suggested in this guide, otherwise, overlapping motifs which appeared and reappeared, and the fact that not everyone was prosperous enough to keep up with minor stylistic influences makes the average collector's task a considerable one. Even museums, unless given exact dates by the donor, generally use at least a decade time span.

Underwear is a good example of difficulty in precise dating.

Much of it was handmade following broad fashion dictates and while seeming to conform to a specific time, can often stem from an entirely different time, so it is best to use the famous 'circa' instead of dealing in specific years.

As 1900 dawned the most memorable thing about the late 1800's left its imprint. It was the shape of the female form. As sleeves continued to grow larger at the top and the skirt narrowed over the hips, the emphasis shifted to the tiny waist. Mention the gay nineties to anyone, the vision it conjures up is invariably that flamboyant, wasp waisted charmer.

4

1879-1880. Left to right, Cashmere dress with crepe; cashmere imported from India. The girl's dress is a copy of adult style, also made of cashmere with grosgrain and lace trim. Note oriental doll and clocks in hose. This dress is of satin with chiffon and velvet; the little girl's coat is velvet with fur trim, bonnet has large, curling feather; the woman's cloak is of heavy silk. This type of dress in excellent condition is almost unattainable, should such costumes become available value can vary considerably dependent upon geographical location and condition. Minimal prices should be $1,500.

These, and the gowns on page 7, are magnificent and feature satin, satin and silk, tulle, grosgrain, fine gauze and faille. Fine examples of the styles of 1880.

Children of 1879-1880. Boy's suit sports large brass buttons both on jacket and pants, the dresses and coats the girls wear are all high priced, very high fashion clothing of the period. Prices vary on any garments of this type but the dresses should begin at $650, $750 for the boy's suit of this era.

PARISIAN FASHIONS OF 1885. Left, walking dress of silk with tiny flower print. Bow trim in back, cut velvet accents. Paris label. Value $1,500 minimum. A very elegant 'dressy' costume of fine wool with lace ruffles on the skirt. Large bustle. Blouse has pleats down front. This was the very latest style in 'fancy' dress in 1885. Paris label. Fan has oriental motif. Value $2,000 minimum. Right, cut velvet trimmed with jet and made to fit over the bustle. Long front panel heavily decorated with jet beads. Lined with silk. The skirt is silk with gold threads and lace insets. Paris label. Should a garment such as this become available with the genuine jet trim it should have a starting price of $2,000. Museums are fast becoming the primary purchasers of this type period clothing.

C. 1885. These ladies wear two piece dresses with pleated skirts, a fairly common fashion at that time. Button trim as well as trimmings of beads and braids were also popular. These dresses are wool, floor length for the older woman, shorter for the younger. Boning in the waists helped minimize the waistline. Value of each $600-750. To contemporary eyes these dresses look quite fussy but often were considered 'house wear.'

Little Lord Fauntleroy had nothing on this young boy who wears a heavily starched white linen and eyelet trimmed collar and cuff set over his suit. Replete with large bow his costume overshadows that of the little girl. Her dress is linen with ruffled yoke and high neckline. The boy's high shoes lace, the girl's button. Collar and cuffs $175-200; girl's dress $200-250.

The flounces, the ribbon and lace inserts, the button trim, the shorter length considered appropriate for the younger woman all point to the style and quality of this dress. Silk and taffeta c. 1884-1885. $600-750.

Although this figured satin dress probably dates from 1894 to 1896, tradition has it that this picture was taken in 1898. This illustrates the continuing fact of life that fashion may dictate a certain style but women wear what they must, or what they love, regardless of 'official judgment.' Value $650-800. Notice lace handkerchief pinned at neckline.

9

Dresses of the 1884-1885 period all reflect excellent workmanship and meticulous detail. Left is rep wool with lace at neck and cuffs. Bottom flounce has small tassels for trim. The secret of this clothing lay in the fit. Standing for fittings was a tedious process. Waist is boned. Value $600-700.
Right has the recurring button trim on a cut velvet over silk bodice. Bottom flounce and of course the front drape gathering to a bustle in back. Value $600-700.

If daisies could tell, this young lady of the 1880's could describe her feelings about the tight corseting of the day which gave gowns such as she wears their unique look. The dress is two shades of satin with a fairly flat bustle. This dress does not sweep the floor. Button trim, lace at high neckline. Value $700-850.

1883 dress, taffeta, ruffled at neck and sleeve edges, fullness at top of sleeve, tight at wrist, self rosettes on circular skirt. Value $400-500.
Man's suit, wool, double breasted, long jacket, high buttoned. Value $275-325.
Child's cotton dress, simple but with ruffled neckline, worn over embroidered-edged petticoat. Value $85-100.

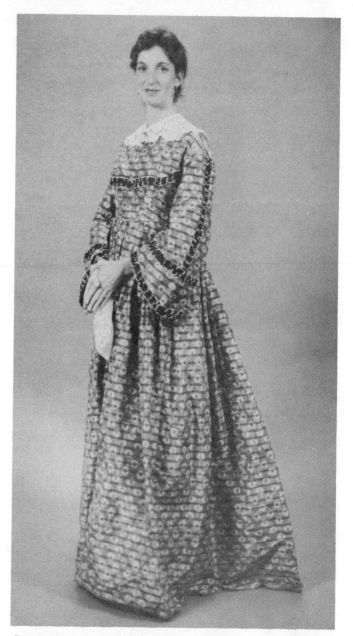

Brown and beige striped taffeta robe, c. 1850-1860, the boned bodice and bell-shaped loose sleeves trimmed with navy and white ruching, the hand stitched skirt lined with brown glazed chintz. Bodice relined at a later date. This robe sold at auction for $400 and is valued at $600-750.

Visiting costume c. 1880. Satin striped brown and lavender satin trimmed with silk patterned in pastel colors and silk fringe. Label: Worth, Worth being the great Parisian couturier. $4,500-6,000.

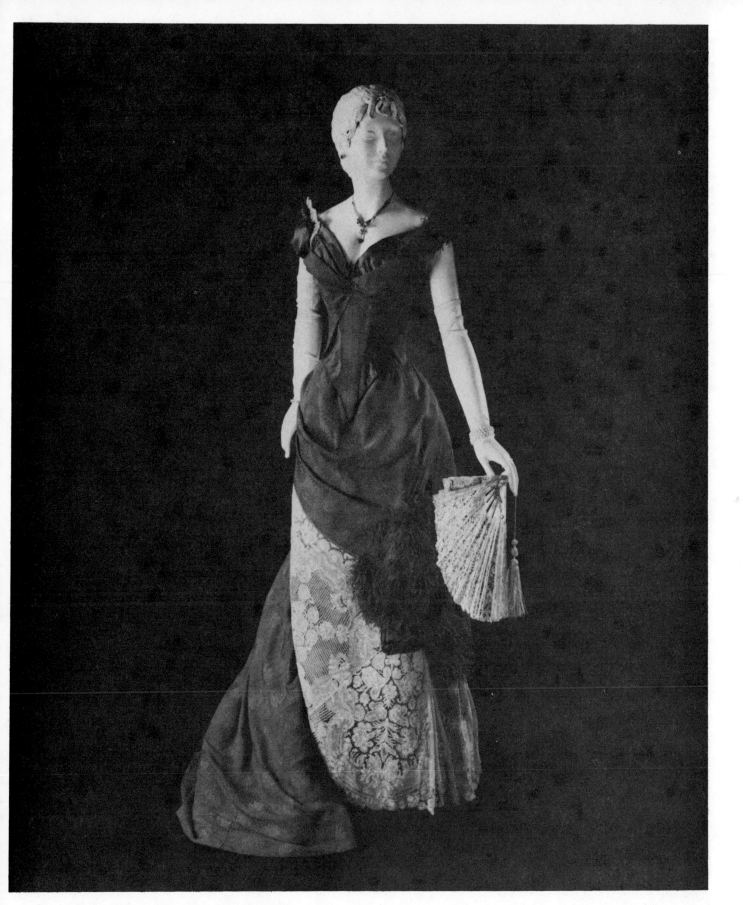

Evening dress by Worth, c. 1885. Crimson figured silk with skirt panel of 18th century point d'Angleterre lace, trimmed with red ostrich plumes. Label. $4,500-6,000. Courtesy of Museum of the City of New York.

C. 1900. Silk Chiffon "one of the fancy new materials" at the turn of the century. Dress, $700-850.

C. 1897-98 straw hat with plumes, $165-200. Wool poplin suit, $450-500. Notice jeweled belt, often these were genuine stones. Kid gloves, French, $30-45.

1894 advertisement. Coats and cloaks of this type are now in the $400-600 range without fur, with fur trim depending on the kind, the price rises at least to the $600-750 range.

1883 Black Mourning dress, gathers in front, ornamented back, trimmed with black jet beads. Value $500-650.

An autumn fete costume, 1894. Cocoa brown with very large leg-o-mutton sleeves. Velvet, striped ribbon trim. Value $700-800.

Latest fashions of 1891. The garment on the left features the very popular ¾ length jacket and the tailored look. The center dress is of silk and the colorful costume reflects the bright and often unusual color combinations worn during this era. The walking dress on the right is of faille and shows the hip detail emphasized during the 1890's. The hats are worn perched squarely on top of the head which was the millinery mode. The shoes were either laced or buttoned and all the ladies wore gloves. Any garment bearing a Paris label of this vintage and obvious quality ranges in price from a minimal $1,750 to 5,000.

Figured silk apricot colored gown, 1890. Value $ 350.-450.
Photo by Kenn Knackstedt. Courtesy Southern Oregon
Historical Society.

1884 Wedding dress. Satin and lace, lace fichu at neck. Value $600-750.
Parasol $155-195.
Photo courtesy of Southern Oregon Museum, Kenn Knackstedt,
photographer.

1880 dress. Black and white characteristic of the second Victorian bustle period. Black velvet fitted bustle jacket, lace dress trimmed with velvet. Black ebony handled parasol trimmed with Spanish lace. Wool hat with cock feathers. Dress, value $600-750 (with jacket). Hat $125-150.

Late 1870's style dress. Made of light blue wool, trimmed with brown velvet. It is accented by a high collared silk blouse. Undergarments consist of a corset and wired bustle. This dress, as shown, is a 1979 copy of an authentic dress in the collection of the State Historical Society of Wisconsin and patterns may be obtained from them. The original pattern has been altered to add the collar, wide cuffs and an extra ruffle to the skirt. Hat is of brown velvet with tinted feathers. Hatbox from Dobbs, Fifth Avenue, NY. Purse is of brown velvet to match the dress.
Costume appraised at $750. Approximate cost of materials $170.

Dark green and amber silk short jacket, high banded neckline of lace over silk, lace bodice. c. 1880-1885. Value $350-400.

Back detail of above photo.

Typical well-dressed couple of the early 1890's. This shoulder and waistline was not just every woman's dream with boning and lacing it was for many an actuality. Fainting was common in those days.

Late Victorian white crocheted house jacket, princess type seams create a beautifully fitted garment. This is photographed on a 1909 patented dress form by Hallborchert Dress Form Co. NY, Chicago. Value of jacket $200-250.

Worth of Paris gown, tussah silk, with train, c. 1898. Known to have been worn in 1900. Value $2,500-3,000.

Victorian blouse with silk corde applique which is different from most blouses of the time. Probably worn with a full skirt with bustle in back. Notice how blouse is cut in back to accomodate the bustle. Tied at waist to form pigeon breasted look. All hand made. Value $400-500.

Victorian combing jacket, machine made lace, silk satin ribbon insets, lined with blue silk. Value $350-450.

21

See-through lace over rust colored taffeta underdress. Known to have been worn about 1890. Value $350-500.

White cambric nightgown, crocheted straps and bodice, tucked and ruffled nightcap. c. 1885.
Nightgown value $150-175. Nightcap value $40-45.

These undergarments of 1893 were called 'waists'. They are rare and make a great sociological comment on the way children were dressed in those years. Left to right, baby's waist worn by infants 1 year old, double V model, ages 1 to 3 years wore this type which in a slightly longer version was worn by boys and girls up to 10 – young ladies ('growing girls') wore this kind until they were 16 – and the ladies wore the extra long waist. This was covered in sateen. These waists supported stockings and underclothes from the shoulder, it supposedly allowed for more freedom of movement. Value $175-200.

Left to right
Princess slip or 'foundation dress'. Shaped to the shoulder by seams to the shoulders front and back. Circular flounce gives round length. This is of lawn but most often these were made of Chinese silk or dimity, worn under the lingerie dresses in vogue in 1910. $195-250. 1910-11. Another princess slip with three ruffles for support of the outer garment. The kind of dresses worn dictated this style of slip. The lower support of flounces gave the dress what was called "the sweep". Value $250-325.    Drawers 1910. Despite the popularity of the combination lingerie, drawers and corset covers continued to be used especially when a 'sheath effect' was not desired. These drawers show a 'yoke belt' finished at the bottom with a deep ruffle which may be either straight or circular. It could be tucked or trimmed with beading or inserted lace. Tape is run through a casing formed by a row of stitching. Embroidery was often used for dainty effect and this affects price. These were an important fashion item at the time and they are most often found in cambric or batiste but they can be found in all qualities some boasting magnificent laces and handwork. Regulation length of these drawers was usually 24" at the side. Price dependent upon materials and trims. Types shown valued at $100-200.

Gentleman's nightshirt, cotton, button front, small pearl buttons, crocheted edging at front and sleeves. c. 1880. Value $100-125.

Elaborate nightdress, c. 1880. Muslin with crochet trim. Value $155-195.

Above
1909. Apron. In 1908-1910 an apron was considered a necessity. "Suitable clothes for the kitchen are as indispensible as the street garb" was the fashion dictate. This apron has a gored skirt to eliminate 'bunching' at the top. It is joined to a waistband and bib portion which fastens at the back by two extensions which button onto the belt. Nurses and housemaids also wore this type apron well into the century. Usually found in gingham, percale, muslin or lawn. Shown in lawn. Value $125-175. As with most everyday type clothing these aprons were often discarded when they showed wear so they are now scarce and still overlooked.

23

Fans typical of the 1890's. Feather fans range between $125-200, lace fans of the type shown $100-175, gauze in combination with other decorative accents $135-155.

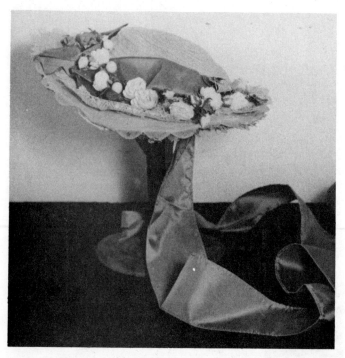

Straw hat, with long taffeta ribbons, floral, ribbon and net trim. c. 1890. Value $125-150.

Parasols, linen, c. 1880. Left, cream linen with blue trim, embroidery. Folding wood handle, still in original box. Value $175-200. Right, tan linen, plain, long wooden handle. Value $95-145.

Millinery trade card of Willis and Dunham of Minneapolis, c. 1870's. This type bonnet was worn for a fairly long period of time. Trade cards are an instructive, very definitive tool in any area of collecting and should always be sought after. The hats are valued at $200-300 in their wonderful shapes and soft straw and floral trim. The trade card cost $24 some years ago.

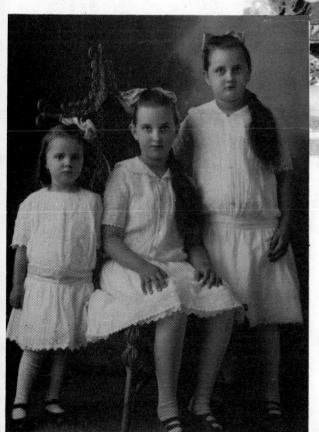

1898. Girls dresses, cotton, belted, scalloped hems and sleeve edges. Value $125-195.

Front and back views of 1882 trade card of Bronner & Co.'s catalogue of Fashions for Spring and Summer. Clothing of this type is almost unobtainable but the price ranges for the garments worn only by the young children in the cart are $50-75 for the hats, boys suit $175-200, girl's dress, $175-200. Older children's outfits, girl's long jacketed suit, value $150-200. Boy's two piece suit, $150-175. High shoes worn by both. Each pair, $55-75. Straw hats, each $50-65.

Boy's fashions, 1867. Courtesy of Butterick Archives.

# BUTTERICK'S PATTERNS FOR BOYS.

64    26    69

64    26    69

156    63    65    154

Hat, straw with satin trim, c. 1898. Value $100-150.

New York fashions of 1871. Courtesy of Butterick Archives.

# CHAPTER TWO
# 1900-1920

The Edwardian era was a long one. It began at the turn of the century and continued until 1910. So the collector can appreciate that although there were modifications of dress and accessories during these years, the tendency is to label all clothing of the period "Edwardian". It has a lovely ring to it and much of the clothing was as elegant and attractive as the classification.

Paris was still the center of fashion and at this fountainhead the wealthy still worshipped.

Actually the clothes of the Edwardian years did not differ significantly from those of the preceding Victorian era.

Frock coats were still correct formal day wear for men, the female waists were still as small as could be managed, and the 'S bend' shape was achieved by tightly laced corsets. There was fullness at the front of the bodice and the skirt was long and bell-shaped. This is one time when emphasis was not on youth, many of the fashion photos and paintings show a mature, full-blown woman.

Although the designation "Edwardian" derived from the years of rule of King Edward of England, the term has become one which encompasses the age of that particular style. The years before 'the war to end all wars' were opulent ones for those who could afford it. The characteristics of the clothing took on the characteristics of the lifestyle; the very large, highly ornamented hats, the high built up hairdo, the standing collar on gowns, feathers, laces and anything else which was thought to enhance the female figure.

Some of the accessories to men's wear, the separate collars in their charming boxes, cuff links and their boxes, collar buttons and their receptacle, all make delightful collectibles.

The whole of fashion was dictated by the way people lived and while lifestyles may alter, fabrics may gain and lose favor, hemlines may go up or down, human habits die hard.

In the early years of the new century, a woman's magazine was noting the carelessness of some women's dress, and complaining about "those careless Cinderellas who go about in curl papers, flappy old wrappers and decrepit shoes through half the day and blossom out in belated splendor toward evening." Today there are those who decry hair rollers in the supermarket and the eternal, uniform tight jeans. Indeed the amusing list of worst-dressed women circulated each year is simply a commentary on one man's opinion of the way celebrities fail the accepted norms of dress. It is always difficult to argue with personal taste and preference is everyone's right, but 'Good Taste Costs No More' as Mr. Gump said and it is interesting that even in today's permissive society you hear echoes of notions of taste which prevailed in the 1900's.

This was a time when the house gown or wrapper became a major part of the average woman's daily life, and very often these were the product of home sewing, or were homemade as the more affluent were wont to label them. These wrappers were so widely used because they were a respite from the torturous corsets, and were loose and comfortable. The less expensive ones were made of calico, percale or flannelette and were made in the same way as the gowns, standing or small collar, cape effects over the sleeves and usually flounced at the bottom of the skirt. These inexpensive items sold for less than a dollar, and now if they can be found they cost $125 and up.

Nineteen hundred was a fairly enlightened fashion time in that it recognized the reality of women's figures, notably that "stout women" were a large segment of the buying public and needed flattering garments. They were frankly referred to in literature of the day as 'plump' and 'stout.' Nowadays there is a distinct trend to satisfying the "large woman" or man. This is a departure for general fashion, some advertisements are featuring size 38 or 40 models, not merely in the abstract to suggest the full figure, but with photographs. Sighs of appreciation can be heard not only from women themselves but from some men who have always found the broomstick silhouette less than inspiring. The 1900's woman had no problems, the 'pigeon breast' was a requirement in clothing.

In the early 1900's America was welcoming immigrants by the thousands, and all were filled with hope. In some ways this cheerful outlook transferred itself to fashion.

The covert skirt and shirtwaist which was a carry over from the 1890's could be worn again and again and interchanged. The mail order catalogues of the 1900's were filled with types of lady's waists, some of them in practical wool flannel. We tend to want to collect the things of rare beauty in clothing and much of what we have left to us is just that, but the ordinary day wear has a homey, well made look and often tells us more about the people and their lifestyles than the more lavish examples. While prices are rising astronomically on the elaborate dresses and gowns, they are going up more slowly on the lesser examples, but going up they are.

The average woman was a practical soul and oftentimes had a real need to buy garments which would give long service. The small standing collar introduced in the 1890's was an integral part of the 1900's scene. 'Wool tricot' was a newly introduced fabric in 1902, the summer dresses were two piece white lawn and were very attractive with their lace, embroidery and ribbon trim. Prices ranged from $3.75 to $6.75, not inexpensive for the time. We tend to think of that period as always incorporating the high banded neckline but the summer frocks were just as apt to be off the shoulder. With the popular bouffant hairdo tied at the nape with the large bows, these styles were quite alluring. Silk waists were expertly made and considered an absolutely necessary part of the wardrobe.

The young children and girls wore carbon copies of the adult clothing except for length which could vary from 20 to 28 inches in children one to five years old. Sailor type waists were in vogue for girls up to 14 years but the wide collar over the shoulder was prevalent.

Men were encased in one or three button cutaway frock coats or the single or double breasted sack which is a straight-lined jacket, and the average width of the pants leg was 22 inches at bottom. It was a neat look, a dandified look, worn with a bowler hat and high collar with bow tie. Surprisingly, many heavy overcoats from that period survive.

They can be found in differing lengths from 42 inches to 52 inches, depending on the height of the wearer, but the 42 inch coat was generally worn short, at knee length.

The cane was standard, and today we see an occasional good cane collection, but overall there are relatively few people collecting them. The umbrellas and canes of the 1900's are quite neglected by the general collecting public. The variety is vast and can keep a collector busy for years. The various material with which the handles were made are endlessly intriguing and often outlasted the cane or umbrella itself. Today we see these relics in the jewelry cases of dealers, and the sterling silver tops are already the subject of serious consideration.

Boys and younger men wore three piece suits for dress, consisting of coat, vest and knee pants which were tight fitting and usually made with 'double knees'. These met high stockings at the knee.

It should be remembered that men's clothing can be striking and expertly made, but currently it is largely the province of museums and costume departments of colleges and theatrical companies. Boys' and men's clothing beautifully round out a diorama or a family scene of mannequins. Not too many collectors have ventured into this field, except for some of the accessories like hats and caps, and this market is bound to make serious price gains.

One of the most important things a serious collector of Vintage Clothing must consider is display. Toward this, it is important to buy older dress forms if possible. If collecting before 1940 is your main focus, buy any dress form you see. In a one dimensional setting the bustle or the train, for example, do not show to advantage but on a dress form all these details are immediately apparent. Here, of course, you compete with many small retailers who are also looking for these forms as elegant display pieces.

The older forms are usually marked with the manufacturer's name and dated, and these are greatly coveted, as are the old wicker which are a challenge to find, the type which can be made small or large, and the ones with iron bases. But buy any form you see until you can buy exactly what you want, so your wonderful old clothes will avoid creasing, folding, and general wear and tear when you take them out to show.

The old wooden hat forms make marvelous background for hats of the period. It is difficult to show a hat collection properly unless the shape and detail can be appreciated and for this you need a hat stand. Although I have uncovered no very large collections of stands, smaller ones abound, and since dealers themselves need them if they carry hats, they are not scarce but are getting harder to find.

Nothing is more beautiful than a hat collection nicely set out, it can be used instead of sculpture, in many ways that is what a well mounted hat resembles. Hats are colorful and different and are a surprising aid to decor.

Some of the hatstands shown in this guide have been found at flea markets and the smaller shops and for the clothing collector it is important to keep in touch with these sources. Some remarkably lovely clothing is turning up this way and recently I purchased a pair of 1920's silk lounging pajamas for much less than the going rate. Basically though, the collector in this field needs to have rapport with a dealer in fine vintage fashion who will supply the kinds of garments in which you are most interested, in good condition.

Decorators, in a sense, are also seeking clothing and accessories of earlier periods to be used to accent a room, and you will find competition from people who have no interest in vintage clothing but have an eye for the unusual. Such a couple has an old life-size corset form, out of a mid-western store, ornamenting their living room. As with all artifacts concerned with vintage clothing, it is a conversation piece. So the clothing collector needs to buy whatever is pertinent to the collection when it is available, this is such a fast-growing field the watchword is haste.

Recently, an exquisite Edwardian silk dress became available through an estate sale. In perfect condition, the price was high. The skirt consisted of much precious material which seemed to flow from a bodice which was boned, but the collector hesitated. After considering it for a few hours, she decided to buy it, but it had been sold. Not too long after, the gown which had the typically low decolletage was spotted at a downtown shop at an even higher price, and it was marked 'sold.'

This is becoming an increasing problem as well as a great boon to the private collector, as more and more shops devoted to Vintage Fashion open and competition becomes keener. It is to the dealer in fine old clothing that the collector should turn for fashions of the Edwardian period. Although the typical dresses and suits are easily recognized, some of the other apparel made between 1900 and 1910 is not so characteristic and it takes a trained eye to identify it. With enough experience, collectors will acquire the same skill.

The Edwardian age fostered a fashion which has never actually disappeared. The shirtwaist look in a modified way has continued to this very day, largely because it is a flattering and easy style. Fashion was still set by the wealthy in 1900-1910 and Paris reigned supreme.

At the turn of the century women wore sweeping skirts and since they did, literally, sweep the floor it must have been a monumental chore to keep clothing immaculate. Around the house, some women resorted to large bands of material folded over the hem and secured on both sides.

Crossing streets and climbing stairs called for lifting the skirt and it was important to do this correctly so as not to disturb the fit over hip and back.

Worth, the incomparable designer and trend setter, was still a famous name and for the fashionable a gown from Worth of Paris was elegance personified.

Furs and feathers, as well as umbrellas and parasols were part of the costume.

Magazines of that time show innumerable ads for underthings and corsets which were considered part of a bride's trousseau and were an important part of the fashionable life of the female. One of the adjuncts to fashion which should appeal to any collector is the boudoir cap which was worn to cover any less than perfect coiffure. These were made in a wide range of materials and trimmings, and are among the delightful fripperies one can search for. While still relatively inexpensive because they have been neglected for a long time, they are rising in price.

Since there are still not too many collectors of these delightful concoctions it is a relatively untapped field, but now their beauty and potential is recognized and a beginning collector should waste no time. About 9 years ago, I purchased a lovely little silk and crocheted cap for $6, several years later I saw a similar cap for almost 6 times that. From an investment standpoint, that is certainly appreciation.

During parts of the Edwardian years, shoes were not always visible, as time went on and skirts shortened, the shoe again became somewhat important. Vintage shoes are becoming expensive and any from this period, either high buttoned or high laced, are quickly sold. The more utilitarian shoes, which were high laced, are almost impossible to distinguish from a man's shoe. Before I began my consuming pursuit of vintage fashion, I bought a pair of what I thought must surely be a man's footwear. A little research showed this to be a woman's shoe, so beware if you are new to period.

It is always wise to look for shoes of the same vintage as the garment, so that when you display you can accompany the dress or suit with the complementary accessories. This gives a sense of completeness, and a sense of history.

The Hobble skirt was prevalent in the years before the first World War, satin shoes for evening and high button shoes for day wear. The flippant "that went out with high button shoes" summed up the reaction of the following decades to that style and that may be why they are so difficult to find. But the shoe collector has a veritable bonanza of choices. Patent leather vamps paired with elegant uppers, sometimes silk or suede, are just waiting somewhere to be discovered.

Of all the collectibles in clothing, shoes seem to attract the fewest fans, although a New York Department store recently had a rather limited showing of vintage designer shoes. Shoes are one of the great indicators of prevailing fashions and often delineate a specific era even more than the garments. Home sewing became widely practiced in the early part of the 20th century and so some fashions could have been made in older styles or clothing could have been altered, but shoes would normally have to be purchased regularly and would thus have been made in the prevailing mode and each time had its typical footwear.

The collector hopes for a pair that is unworn, but this is not always possible, and even museums are now resigned to showing shoes that are in less than perfect condition. High button shoes, especially those belonging to small children have an endearing quality that shoes of other periods do not possess, and of course there are those shoe button hooks which come in several sizes and have attractive handles, often silver or mother-of-pearl. Try for a few of these to match the shoes. Try always to think of your collectible in the round; the shoe button for the right shoe style; the appropriate stand for the hat; the dress form to show off the gown; the correct handbag, all of these can give meaning to your clothing. Visit your local museum or an available Vintage Clothing Museum (such museums are proliferating rapidly) or even a fine Vintage Clothing shop to see how the professionals do it. Any collection benefits from being complete and it is the small things which lend interest. The Smithsonian Institution is now placing emphasis on the background of the First Ladies' gowns. As well as the gowns themselves, the display is moving to include period rooms and accessories.

The hats had to be spectacular to accommodate the coiffure, and a long hatpin was needed. Hatpins are an almost legendary collectible and are often classed with jewelry, but I feel that those who love the Edwardian era should collect a few representative hatpins. A simplistic rule of thumb has it that the older the hatpin the longer the shaft and this is usually true, after all it had to pierce hat, hair, rats, padding and heaven knows what else. Hatpins, which were costing only a few dollars a few years ago can now go for astronomical prices depending on age, the kind of metal used as well as the genuineness of the stones, and beauty.

Of special interest during the 1900-1910 period were the hats men wore. A man's hat, you may say, is just a hat. Not true, even today when hats are seldom worn, notice the caps men are donning with more frequency; baseball caps, caps with company logos, caps with club emblems, usually vented on top and back for summer comfort, and peaked. In warm areas of the country these caps are becoming commonplace. In 1900 the top hat went with the frock coat, the homburg was becoming necessary to the less formal day suit and the straw hat became the fancy of both men and women.

Just as the fashions of women have moved to the less formal, the coats and caps of the gentlemen who drove their motorcars were for those times, fairly informal. In fact, the motorcar was beginning to change America and Americans.

It was in 1913 that a revolutionary change altered women's clothing. It was the V-neck and we can only imagine the freedom that must have brought to the 1900's woman. It was avant-garde for the time and not everyone immediately rushed into it, and the shirtwaist and gored skirt persisted. Silk stockings were worn and on shirts of sheer batiste sparkled crystal or rhinestone buttons. Cotton voile was the choice for day dresses, it was dainty and figured, and lined in a "suitable color."

By 1915 skirts began to widen considerably at the hem but remained tight at the hips. The high waist, raised as much as 2½ inches above normal gave a long line to the skirt, and the voluptuous, mature ideal of the first decade of the 20th century was phasing out.

The years from 1900 to the outbreak of World War I were a time of extravagance and ostentation. The balloon sleeves of the 1890's disappeared and were now tight and extended halfway down the hand. The function of clothing was more practical, how could they have functioned in their overdone, elaborate clothing, as they left the home for shops and offices it was evident that clothing was going to have to adapt to the woman instead of woman adapting to the dictates of fashion.

It was this era that gave us the Gibson girl with the hour glass figure and we can probably forgive fashion arbiters for almost anything just for the pleasure of looking at her. Charles Dana Gibson's creation was the epitome of female beauty of her day, and so lovely that even now, with a few alterations, she can be considered the model for full-blown beauty. Her intricate pompadour coiffure, her gorgeous exposed shoulders by night and her trim fitting neckline by day, coupled with her hour glass figure and provocative poses, decorate more walls of nostalgia buffs than one can count even in this jeans and tee-shirt age. One of the world's best kept secrets is the 'Gibson Man' but attractive as he was, he obviously didn't have that special something.

The late years of the decade were geared toward making the 'World Safe for Democracy.' Simple lines had replaced the former constricting clothing and by the time the men returned home from the trenches they must have suffered a culture shock – they had left a nation of females mincing about in long hobble skirts and now found the vision of women in skirts just below the knee. Women who had participated in the war effort began to forsake the clothes which limited their activities. Realization had arrived that there were things to do, women could do them, but the garments had to fit the dream.

That war changed not only fashion, it changed the entire world forever.

What is fashion anyway? It is probably the ultimate manifestation of a basic need, to be warm, to impress, or as some anthropologists would have it, an early need to be better than the animals. Whatever it is, the clothing collector daily gives thanks.

The average woman has probably not often had the desire to be dressed by a great couturier. Indeed it would be superfluous to her way of life, so it has always been the leisured class which has made fashion. True, the designs filtered down so what we buy off the rack can certainly be traced to an original made in Paris, or Ireland, or Italy but there are hordes of women whose main aim is to look attractive and depending on the occasion, alluring or competent.

Men have been locked into the business type clothing for so long that today any changes taking place are influenced by television. Men's cosmetics, colognes, high heeled boots, brighter colors – Louis the XIV would be right at home with the coming revolution in men's fashions. Some women are no doubt as startled to see these alterations in men's fashions as the returning service men were to see the short skirts of 1919, men have taken to the sports shirt and jacket and in many circles, academia is one, there is less emphasis on the tie; and the hat for purposes other than warmth, is a thing of the past.

Nineteen twenty marked more than the end of a decade, the coiffure was beginning to sport the permanent wave, shorter skirts and more slender figures with a less defined waistline had somehow evolved. Women had the vote, they were moving into the workforce in numbers and their clothes were becoming less restricted and more utilitarian. It was a far cry from Women's Lib, but the signs were there, and as usual fashion foreshadowed the future.

Lingerie dress, white, 2 piece. Waist has ruffles, sleeves have inset lace. Inserts and trim on skirt ruffles match those on waist. Value $350-450. 1910-1915. Parasol is small size silk with lace, velvet and flower trim. Value of parasol $175-200.

Lingerie dress, 1920's. White sheer cotton inset with wide bands of Irish crochet lace. $600-1,000. This beautiful garment is from the auction of actress Ruth Gordon's clothing held in New York in 1986 by William Doyle Galleries. The pre-auction estimate was $300-500, it not only went over estimate but it was a bargain at the price. Since clothing auctions are proliferating, do not neglect them.

Left to right: Tea gown, c. 1915, of black dotted white silk gauze with high-necked yoke of lace. Peacock blue silk sash, black velvet bow trimming in hobble skirt style. Value $350-500
Two piece summer dress, white linen bodice and skirt with eyelet embroidery, c. 1900. Value $350-450.
Summer dress of mauve and white striped cotton voile with square collar. Value $300-350.
Linen suit. Ecru and lace, two piece, linen, with matching embroidered parasol. Value of both $500-750.

Silk ecru skirt with bustle in back drawn up with a ribbon. Ecru battenberg blouse trimmed in black velvet, rhinestone buttons. Hat is also battenberg with velvet and rhinestone (brilliants) trim. Skirt value $175-225. Waist $350-400, Hat $125-165.

33

**Summer** toilette, c. 1900. Black and white striped silk, chiffon and machine made Alencon lace fichu, lace engageantes (trim at sleeve ending), black satin trim. Label: Worth. Value of this striking ensemble $3,500-4,500.
Any Worth of Paris labeled dress should begin at a minimal $2,500, if in good condition.    Museum of the City of New York

Jacquard silk with French lace revers, appliqued embroidery, French rosettes, mauve with purple velvet sash, square buttons, C. 1910, value $300-450. Woman's straw hat, c. 1910, $95-125.

C. 1900 gown, brown handkerchief linen, inset lace. A magnificent dress. $450-650.

Calico morning dress or wrapper, c. 1900. Square collar, rounded yoke, ruffles at shoulder. Skirt has wide flounce at ankle. Made from a contemporary pattern. Value of original in period, $175-200. Photo courtesy of FOLKWEAR, San Rafael, CA.

Afternoon dresses, 1913. Waistline at almost natural level. Left, satin dress with draped skirt and jacket effect over chiffon chemisette. Tight sleeves. Value $400-450. Afternoon dress. Draped skirt revealing underskirt of silk to match silk jacket and lining of dress. Dress has double line of buttons decorating front. Value $400-500.

This is the stylish overblouse effect, 1916. The skirt is circular and the girdle is wide satin. Value $395-425. Chemise tunic dress, tunic is one unbroken piece from shoulder to hem. Neck has a turnover collar at back and sides. Value $395-425.

Left: One piece 'calling' gown. The blouses were by now fairly plain and this is typical. It has a front closing and plain sleeves. The neck is trimmed with a wide epaulette collar. The skirt is four gores and opens in front and is attached to the blouse. These rather simple dresses were considered appropriate for almost any time of day and released women from changing their clothing so often. This is very fine serge. Value $300-350. Notice the length of the bag strap. Right: Youthful frock has simple blouse made with drop shoulder and has a small full vest in front. Three gored skirt has a narrow front panel of contrasting material. This dress is wash-silk. 1912. Value $300-325.

Left, a dainty figured cotton voile dress worn over an underslip of contrasting color. In these sheer fabrics a contrasting colored undergarment was considered fashionable and "care should always be taken that the underwear does not show through". The blouse closes a little left of center, it has the drop shoulder and a plain sleeve. The neck has a small, shaped collar. The skirt is three gored with a high waistline and a soft girdle hides the joining of waist to skirt. Value $300-375.

Center, This dress reflects "the dignity of plainness." Although this shirtwaist 'waist' and five gored skirt which fastens in back does not seem too austere to our eyes it had none of the highly esteemed trims so favored. It was considered a good style for 'mourning' clothes of the period, in a suitably muted color, of course. Value $300-350.

This is a smart coat-costume. The coat is actually a blouse and forms the waist of the dress without the use of any other bodice beneath it. The deep neck opening accomodates a chemisette. The sleeves are cut in one with the body of the coat and the peplum below the belt gives the cutaway effect. The tailoring on much clothing of this period is quite sophisticated. Value of costume with skirt of linen and coat of satin and crepe, $350-400.

Above right:

1914. This Spring model is all wool French serge. This dress is designed with a detachable shadow lace yoke and collar. The collar is in a new shape embroidered and elaborated with Honiton effect braid. The vestee is trimmed with lace frill and small crystal buttons. The skirt is draped gracefully with self-covered buttons. Navy blue embroidered in white. Very attractive dress. Value $450-650.

Afternoon gowns. Left to right: C. 1910. Calling costume, 2 piece, blouse is gathered along the shoulder seam in the front and the fullness thus falls loosely about the figure. It is gathered at the belt. V-neck which could be filled with a small chemisette and standing collar. 2 piece skirt fits snugly but at the lower opening of the side seam there is a slit which displays the petticoat. Value $275-325. 2 pieces. The blouse is gathered along the shoulder seam in front and along the lower edge of a shoulder yoke in back, which gives a soft, droopy effect. The skirt is a plain peg top style with a little fullness in front but the back is flat in the upper part with a bulge below the hips then again flattens. Recommended for a slender or medium figure. $300-325. 3rd from left: For morning wear. Bodice built on shirtwaist lines but is given a decorative touch by the very low drop shoulder and the yoke which is straight and is used only in front. Sleeve is plain at the shoulder but wide at the armhole where it is set in and slightly full where it joins the cuff at the wrist. Narrow skirt with sash. Morning wear demanded simplicity. Value $250-275. 4th from left: For the Matinee or Afternoon Tea. Plain blouse opens in front, skirt has three gores which gives a seamless back and center-front closing. Value $295-350. Two models wear high button shoes, two wear pumps with buckles.

Early winter styles of 1912-1913. The coat blouse was popular and the model at left shows small V shaped opening at neck, single pointed revers; side and back have a wide ornamental collar, worn with a chemisette. Sleeve fits the arm snugly with no fullness at shoulder. The blouse has a peplum which hangs over front and sides of skirt. The skirt is narrow at the hem. Wool rep with small figures, trimmed with white. Value $300-450.

This model is 'dressy' and has the drop shoulder which by late 1913 was almost a fashion requirement. It also has the loose sleeve without any fullness at the shoulder. Sleeves are widely cuffed at the elbow, the neckline is a shallow V with which a chemisette was not strictly necessary. The edges of the neck opening are trimmed with small sharply pointed revers faced with brocaded velvet. The closing is in front. Five gore skirt opens to display a narrow panel of brocaded velvet which produces a slash effect without an actual opening. These fancy dresses show a remarkable sophistication and were intended for matinee, for calls, and for afternoon wear in general. Value $300-450.

The hats of 1913 can be safely described as overwhelming.

Left: Waist is of gray drap in the Directoire style. It has a silk lining, when joined to a skirt it forms a semi-princess line. 3/4 length sleeves. Satin and lace. Value $350-400.

Right: Intended for the larger woman this waist is of old-rose crepe meteor with a square neckline with tucked insert, ruff chemisette. Satin sash, chiffon sleeves. Value of chemisette $150-175. Value of waist $300-350.

2 piece dress, 1915. Overblouse and girdle with an underblouse of satin with frilled neckline. Velvet and satin. Value $350-450. Coat, loose sports coat or 'college coat.' Sacque cut (which means without a break from the shoulder to the hem.) Value $200-250.

A summer dress reflecting the popularity of bordered materials. The blouse has the then-new style kimono shoulder and closes in the back. Square neckline. The skirt is a one piece model with a straight lower edge and is laid in folds around the waistline. Silk. Value $600-700. Notice the distinctive standing feathers and bows on the hats. The parasol was carried as a regular accessory.

1914. The silhouette of 1914 was flattering and rather sensuous. This dress has a vestee effect, flat collar, drop shoulders, tunic over tighter skirt, pointed shoes just visible. Long sleeves with chiffon ruffles are very kind to the hands. Dress is of silk. Value $400-500.

Spring of 1915 was a flattering time for the female figure. The looser easier fashions were very feminine. These two dresses are typical and are good examples of the length of the clothes as well as the hats. Fashions such as these of good quality and in excellent condition are valued at $500-750.

A 'wash' dress for summer. In the period 1910-1911 the soft look for summer was considered modest and proper since petticoats could then be worn underneath. This skirt is batiste and is attached to a waist of the same material. Trim is Valenciennes lace which in those days was considered inferior to Cluny, Maltese or Irish laces. Skirt is five gored lengthened by a flounce. Dainty bag and hat with large silk roses complete the outfit. Value of dress in this very desirable material and the favored white $500-750.

The variety of skirts and blouses of this period is almost infinite yet not enough survive intact to satisfy demand. This waist indicates the beauty, femininity and marvelous design work in clothing of this period. A very jaunty style indeed is this waist which closes on the left side with buttons under a row of fancy braid. The lower round neck is complemented by the chemisette in ruff style. Tucked to waistline. Sleeves are one seam leg-o-mutton, trimmed at the wrist. Chemisette is organdy finished with lace. Often these chemisettes are found separately and not recognized. The skirt is striped cheviot, considered a walking skirt and might very well be worn under a coat similar to that shown in coat group. Value of chemisette $150-175, value of skirt $225-250, value of waist $295-375.

Waist and skirt outfits. Both waists are made to be adapted to either separate skirt or to be attached to a skirt and worn as one garment. Worn with belts, high round standing collars and appropriate hats. Entirely typical of the 1909-1910 era. Blouse on left is worn with contrasting colored skirt to make a shirt-skirt outfit, waist on the right worn with matching skirt to give the appearance of a dress. Both belt buckles would be highly collectible in themselves. Value of waists of this type $250-300. Value of skirts $195-225. Complete outfit value $700-850.

Often the skirt and waist combination was an elaborate affair but practical clothes were important for general use. This skirt was made for everyday use, its overall line is the sheath effect with a fullness at the lower edge. 7 gore skirt with tuck, close fitting in a 'clearing' or walking length. Broadcloth. Value of skirt $200-250.

Center: 1911. Blouse or waist with narrow tucks stitched in pointed yoke effect front and back, lined with silk, leg-o-mutton sleeves, simple flat collar, chiffon with satin bow. Waist value $195-250. Walking skirt, nine gores, seams lapped and doubly stitched. Has what was called the 'clearing length'. Graceful. Linen. Worn with belt. Value $200-250.

Right: 1911. Waist and skirt. By 1910 the new skírts were being made with a high waistline and shirts or waists were being made to be adaptable for the ordinary style or the newer Empire line. This waist shows the Empire influence with the bodice being made over a French lining which is faced for the chemisette and should the waist be attached to a skirt in high-waist effect this lining serves as a bodice stay. The waist is tucked in panel effect front and back, left side front closing. Soft silk, value of waist and skirt $500-600. Hat value $200-250. The skirt shows the lengthening of lines and softening of skirt lines and is semi-princess, six gores, sheath fitted having a panel in front and a seam on each hip. High waisted button closing. This kind of skirt could also be had with the then newest trailing effect, the short train.

43

Left: Misses' one piece dress for summer or travelling. This kind of dress was also considered correct for beach wear. This is of linen, hand embroidered, the coat is basically plain held in at the waist with a belt, neck has a small turnover collar, notice lack of fullness in the sleeves. This was intended for the teenager. Value $250-350. Right: Another dress for the young miss. This is a one piece garment combining comfort and style. The blouse has a tuck at the shoulders, wide collar, elbow length sleeves ending in a cuff. Three gore skirt opens in the center front. The usual buttons. Notice the towering decorations on the deep brim hats. Value of dress $200-300.

Left: Coat-suit for a young girl of 1912. The coat is quite long reaching near knee length. Resembles the Norfolk style with a deep yoke in front and back and below this the material is tucked or pleated leaving the center front plain. Notched collar with small revers faced in plaid. The sleeve is plain. Five gore skirt is adjusted snugly to the figure all around. It was considered more stylish to have this costume made in two different materials, the jacket for example would be plain and the skirt plaid. This was considered economical as well as fashionable for then the jacket could do extra duty. Value of suit $400-500. Right: Young girl's dress for general wear. The blouse has a square yoke which was coming into vogue in late 1912 with no yoke in back. This dress has a modified V neck with a turnover collar. This was termed the 'medici effect'. Sleeves are plain at the shoulder and gathered at wrist with a deep cuff. Skirt is three gored, cut to give a tunic effect. Chevior serge, value $200-300.

Left to right: The very fashionable vest in the summer dress of 1915. Three gore skirt has a yoke in front and on the sides. Ribbon trim runs in an unusual way through loops on the top of waist. Muslin. Value of these 'pretty' dresses is rising. $400-450. The waist of this dress buttons up the front to a wide flat collar. Frilled. The skirt is three gored and is joined to the yoke with a belt. Both skirt and waist are cotton. Value $300-350. The waist of this dress is made with the body and sleeve in one piece. It is worn over a guimpe. Skirt is in one piece and has scalloped outines for placing the ruffles. Figured lawn in a very soft, feminine style. Notice the continued use of the parasol which is making a comeback today to ward off the sun. Value of this dress is $600-700. These dresses are typical of 1915 with the increasing emphasis on the soft look and comfort. The dress on the right has the 'new' Quaker collar. Value of these types of dresses depends on materials, details and appeal. Range is $350-750.

In 1915 no dress was complete without the fancy collar which could be wide or narrow, high in the back for a long neck opening or shallow with the little collar. This is a cross section of various types of collars popular in the summer of 1915. Occasionally these collar and cuff sets are found intact.

Left to right: Some of the very attractive fashions of 1915. A 4 gore model skirt has attached suspender trim made of straight pieces of velvet ribbon. Worn with a simple blouse. Skirt value $195-250. The blouse of this dress has an open neck with small collar and long tapering revers. Front forms a panel passing over the belt. Three gore skirt attached to the blouse without fullness. Pongee. Value $250-300. Popular middy blouse (which is still a legitimate fashion). Lacing on sides, sailor collar. Cotton. Value $125-150. Shirtwaist dress, loose untrimmed blouse closes in surplice style. These pieces which can be considered 'separates' are valued separately. Blouse $125-195, skirt $150-175. This blouse has the bolero effect. The skirt is gathered at the top. Figured lawn. Value $350-400. This is one of those dresses every collector tries for. Silk with the soft feminine look. Shorter hair, attractive shoes, 1915 was a good year for fashion. Value of this dress is $600-750.

46

Left to right: 1915 afternoon wear. The waist on the left is considered to be in the 'military style.' The sleeve is the 'bishop' which is simply a sleeve plain at the shoulder and slightly full at the wrist. The skirt is circular. The dress value is $300-350.

A good example of the surplice-style waist. This is made of lace flouncing with a guimpe (underblouse) of chiffon which has the high collar although this was no longer so popular. Long loose sleeves. Skirt is a one piece model, tucked. A very wide girdle. Value $500-600.

A jumper type dress with a one piece circular skirt. The jumper-like top is considered an 'overblouse'. The underblouse is messaline, the dress is silk with an extremely wide girdle sash. Value $500-600.

Left: Directoire Princess dress, foulard silk, the waist has square yoke of net with a band of embroidered net, four large self-covered buttons, entire sleeve is made of net, a rather usual thing in that period, shaped net collar. The skirt reflected the new mode which was to hang gracefully from the hips, stitched belt attaches the skirt to the waist. Silk was not an unusual material in the most popular dresses of that day. Value $300-325.

Right: 1909. Princess jumper dress, taffeta silk in wisteria color, front of waist is trimmed with soutache braid which gives panel effect, skirt designed in the new style and is trimmed down the center with a row of taffeta silk covered buttons, braid trimmed belt attaches skirt to waist and fastens in back. Value $300-325.

1915. Lustrous silk was widely used for evening dresses as well as dresses for the house. This is a waist and skirt dress made of silk with the drop shoulder and small standing collar. Value $450-500.

Typical shirtwaist styles of the first decade of the 1900's. Value of each of the blouses. $350-450. Value of each of this type skirt, $200-275. Price depends on quality and trim.

Right: 1910. Dressy waist of fine quality ecru net over Japanese silk; front is embroidered in floral design and trimmed with tucks, rows of wide and narrow lace insertion and lace edging, rows of lace insertion give a short round yoke effect in back. Full length tucked sleeves with pointed cuffs, trimmed with lace insertions, tucked with trimmed collar, fastens in back. Notice the buckled belt. Value $350-400.

Left: Another waist of the period, dressy style in messaline silk trimmed in front with Venise and Valenciennes lace edging, lace collar, full length shaped sleeves trimmed with lace insertions and edging. Value $350-400.

1912. A soft, graceful afternoon gown. The blouse is scarcely fitted at the shoulders and the balance of the front and back is soft and loose. The sleeve is attached without fullness and makes a soft puff at the wrist where there is a frill. At the neck is a square collar and joining the lower edges of this are two scarf-like insertions forming a fichu effect. The drape of the skirt is called the 'Turkish style' and suggests harem wear. Raised waistline and drapery over the hips. The front small skirt opening is filled in with chiffon, the gown is crepe de chine. Satin sash. An outstanding dress, value $500-650. Notice the buckles on the shoes.

A high waisted semi-princess dress. This style was prevalent during the 1909-1911 period. Made of sateen with velvet trim and soutache braid. Value $400-500.

1909 House dress, sometimes called 'morning dress'. Tucked blouse-waist closes down front side on left making it easier to put on or take off, band facing on the waist is made with high neckline, long sleeves. Linen with striped band trimming. Value $400-450.

Semi-princess dress with normal waistline. A basic lingerie dress in soft linen with satin trim. Bodice not lined, button trim. Simple construction of deep V neck shirt, skirt has short train. Value $400-425.

1905 Gibson Girl silhouette and coiffure. Outfit, $450-600.

1905 Young ladies' outfit, $350-550.

Semi-princess lingerie dress. These dresses had no blouse lining. This is fine lawn trimmed with Valenciennes insertions and edgings. In buying dresses of this type it is important to note the compatibility between the openings of the waist and skirt which must be at the same point either center back or side. White lawn. Value $400-425.

Cream serge dress, 1913. Bodice is deep U filled in with yoke of lace and moire taffeta. Skirt narrows at ankle. Value $300-325. Young girl's dress; 2 piece skirt with tunic overdress. Wide panels front and back and belted. Linen, value $100-135. Plain waist and skirt, shirtwaist type. Neckline trimmed with notched collar and is closed in the duchesse style in the center front. Skirt closes in the front. Waist is Japanese silk with satin trim. Value $295-325. Another shirtwaist dress, 1913. Plain waist, striped, unusual sleeve which continues in a point to the edge of the collar. Skirt is four gore, closing at the left side of the back, belted. Usually these waists are made of pongee silk and skirts of light woolen goods, serge or cheviot. Value $250-275.

Left to right: Everyday dresses, winter. 1915. Shirtwaist dress, printed crepe de chine, high neck with gathers. Skirt is of mixed cheviot. Value $345-375. Raglan sleeve blouse with tunic skirt. Matching underskirt. Value $300-350. The popular overblouse, worn with long sleeved waist. Tunic skirt. Chiffon, silk and satin trim. Value $400-450.

51

Left to right: Sports coat worn with 3 piece skirt for every day wear. Wool plaid skirt, solid color cheviot jacket with wide belt and self-covered buttons. Two large pockets. Skirt buttons down front. Skirt $95-125 in excellent condition without moth holes, coat which can be buttoned to neck is valued at $150-175, again in excellent condition.

This dress exhibits the 'drop shoulder'. It closes in the front. The skirt is 2 pieces with a 3 piece yoke. Skirt narrows considerably at the hem. An easier style becoming evident in 1914. Value in silk $400-450.

Semi-fitting, full length coat with broad revers and velvet collar and cuffs. Cheviot. Leather handbags were popular at this time. Coat $200-225. Coats are not widely collected and still undervalued.

Vests were extremely fashionable at this time and in this dress the vest which is of the same material as the collar, extends below the belt. The 3 piece skirt is topped with a satin sash. This dress is worn with a lace chemisette. The sashes are not usually found with these dresses unless they were attached. Value of dress in silk $450-500.

Easy to slip on dress for everyday wear in 1914. Skirt is six gores, blouse is simply styled with side buttoning and flat collar in contrasting color. Chiffon ruffle at wrists. Value $300-350.

Misses' dresses, 1915. Considered a youthful style, this blouse and skirt has a bordered skirt and a blouse whose collar can be worn flat or arranged to close in high necked style. Sleeve fullness is gathered into the band cuff. Skirt has a deep round at the front. Serge. Value $250-275. Right: Overblouse worn with a plain waist, which again has a convertible neck. Bishop sleeves with wide cuff. Skirt, 2 piece, circular cut. Usually found in fine serge with chiffon or net, or velvet and wool. Value $175-250. Today it is difficult to determine that these were worn by young women since the sizes are large.

Home garments: left to right: 1912. Semiprincess style, for home wear, sateen. $150-175. Child's apron. Sacque style, fastens in back, has ties extending from side seam, roll collar and long sleeves. Figured lawn. Value $65-85. House dress, morning wear. Has patch pocket and some sleeve fullness at shoulder. Cotton crepe. Value $150-175. Russian suit for young boy. Coat closes over at side standing collar, sleeves have little fullness and band cuff. Pants are made without a fly. Linen. Value $185-200. Maternity dress. This is attached to a lining which is adjustable. Drop shoulders and plain sleeves. Lightweight silk. Value $200-275.

Afternoon dresses, 1913. Frock for young girl. Light and dark fabric, buttons down front, five gored skirt. Value $285-300. One piece Empire dress. Striped silk. Value $300-325. Shirtwaist costume of tan cotton pongee with white linen collar and cuffs. Value $285-300. White serge afternoon dress, black satin trim, value $325-350.

Right: Shirtwaist design with four gored skirt of 1913. Box pleated with collar and cuffs of contrasting material. Front closure, buttons from collar to hem. Tan pongee with green and white satin trim, green glass buttons. Value in silk with original buttons $300-350.

Left: 1913. This is a morning dress in a simple style. Gingham with collar and cuffs of dotted lawn. The blouse is ornamented with a fancy collar and cuffs. No sleeve fullness at the shoulder. The three piece skirt fits snugly and has left side opening, pocket. Value $250-275.

Left to right: Ladies' House dresses, 1916. Simple style, button front, small collar, bishop sleeves (plain at the shoulder and gathered into a cuff at the wrist). Usually found in washable fabric. Value $145-185. Apron, serviceable work apron, front panel fitted, gingham, value $40-60. House dress, side closing waist, 7 gore skirt. Cotton. Value $135-155.

Costumes for home wear: 1915. Left: ladies' bath robe, flannel or wool. Not too many robes of this type survive. Value $50-75. Right: House dress, 2 piece, plain blouse with center front closing. Skirt has 3 gores and is gathered at the top, the sides and the back. These were usually made of washable material, and occasionally in wool. Value $125-150.

An overview of the fashions of 1919, top left is a cotton, one-piece house dress $100-125; two variants of the waist, value ranges $95-150; three dresses typical of the daywear which range in value from $200-450 depending on material, trimmings and overall appeal. A good example of the skirts which were made in 2, 3, or 4 pieces. Value range $200-250 because these are difficult to find.

Misses' Silk Gowns
Advance Spring Models

Women's Silk Gowns
Advance Spring Models

1916. Misses' taffeta silk and georgette gown in old rose, with hand embroidered bodice and sleeves in self color, vestee of georgette crepe, tunic skirt with panel front of taffeta and georgette crepe which is hand embroidered, crushed girdle of taffeta silk. Gorgeous dress $700-800. Shoes are tan Russian calf laced boots. 1916. Misses' changeable armure taffeta silk gown in blue, bodice and standing collar embroidered in self color, sleeves and vestee of georgette crepe full flare skirt with peplum and girdle of silk. Both high shoes and pumps were fashionable. Dress $700-800. Model wears white buckskin pumps with self bows. For the more mature woman a taffeta silk gown in black, vestee of lace and embroidered georgette crepe, georgette crepe sleeves with gauntlet cuffs of taffeta, pointed tunic skirt with bands of velvet ribbon. Value $700-800. White kid boots with Havana brown kid backs. Women's taffeta silk gown in navy blue with georgette crepe sleeves finished with taffeta cuff, the then-new 'Spanish collar' and vestee of white net, girdle of georgette crepe with bands of taffeta silk. Value $700-800. She wears patent kid slippers with hand-sewed shell ornament.

Beaded black lace evening gown, c. 1915, in tunic style with long sleeves, black furred trained hem, cream satin underslip, the lower tunic bodice and sleeves decorated with crystal and jet beading the central bodice panel has rhinestone and coral decoration, later applied, some renovation to interior. Even with these deficiencies the gown sold at the recent Butterfield auction for $425 and restored is worth $680-850.

Cream and Black Lace Evening Gown, c. 1905, black Chantilly lace bodice and short sleeves appliqued with black and cream sequined design, the full trained skirt similarly embroidered, cream taffeta underslip later replaced. The estimated pre-sale auction value was $300-500. This gown sold for $1,200 and given its quality is worth much more.

Center, c. 1915 silk evening gown of orchid satin, the trained skirt with center chiffon panel, gold lace and velvet trim, crossover bodice and sleeves of pale blue chiffon similarly trimmed, taffeta lining. Shows some wear but a gorgeous gown. Value $500-600.
Left: c. 1915 powder blue satin evening gown, the skirt has two front flying panels, short black net sleeves are trimmed with black jet beads, flying side panels of black net are similary trimmed, black, blue and rhinestone beaded, appliqued central front panel decoration, cream taffeta lining, which is a replacement. Value $400-450.
Right: c. 1915-16 deep burgundy velvet skirt, bodice of pleated chiffon and gold lace, ornate rhinestone decoration on the bodice, burgundy pleated underslip. Value $400-450.

Formal gold dress with train. Trimmed with lace and jet beads and completely lined except for train. Yellow pearl buttons. Worn about 1900. Black lace ball fan. Value, dress $350-450.

1906. Formal gown of black velvet. Overskirt drapes in front and back with tassels of sterling silver and velvet. Sleeves and bodice are heavy but fine Continental lace. Value $500-600. Black velvet hat with large ostrich plumes and with pin which matches belt buckle on dress. Marcasite. Value of hat $145-175.

Typical gowns of 1909-1910. Meticulous attention to detail, fitted with trims of laces, satin insets and chiffon and other expensive, elaborate materials. These gowns were considered to be all that the well-dressed woman could want – the total costume reflected the finished product of cosmopolitan progress. The clinging, trailing gowns were described as a "beautiful vase holding one perfect flower." What woman could resist that image? Gowns of this quality, beauty and workmanship are scarce and desirable. Value $1,500-3,000.

Typical waist and skirt outfits of the 1909-1911 period. Worn with round high collars they are Empire style, with semi-princess lines. The skirt falls softly and has a train. The skirt on the right has 'clearing' for walking. Costumes of this type are valued at $450-550 with the 'train' models usually commanding more.

Evening gown of pink chiffon trimmed with pink ribbon and silk Teneriffe wheels. High neck, deep bertha forms cape over sleeves. 1904. Value $650-850.

Walking suit of ecru linen c. 1910. Skirt has long yoke and wide pleats. Long pocket. $400-500. Straw hat with plaid ribbons $40-50.

Two piece black afternoon suit of wool with train. Revers trimmed with braid, ribbed dickey is satin. Top is boned with small stand-up collar. Early 1900's. The wool in this suit is very fine. Value $600-750. Victorian flat hat of sealskin with ribbons down back and chin strap. Value $100-150; ostrich boa of Victorian vintage. Value $275-300.

Brown wool, 2 piece dress with braid worked into the waist, the sleeves are decorated with very dainty, pretty old glass buttons. 1890-1900. The yoke of the dress snaps into the jacket which also has matching buttons. Value $600-750. Brown straw hat with pale coral silk flowers.

This skirt is not gored but is circular. The skirt is worn with a coat for a suit effect. Closure is buttoned to hem. Medium sweep in 'clearing length' for walking. Serge. Value of skirt with jacket, $550-750. Parasol of linen, value $175-195. Parasol values continue to rise.

1910. Tailored suit intended for Spring wear. The ultimate daytime wear for the Howard Chandler Christy girl. Not only is her suit in the latest mode with the long cutaway jacket, her hat is a masterpiece of the milliner's art and her handbag is the silver mesh with chain handle so collectible today. Buckles on her pointed toe shoes, the dress shows enough ankle to be tantalizing. Suit $450-600, hat $200-250, bag $100-125.

1913 poplin walking suit. Worn for travelling, visiting, shopping, etc. Trimmed with lighter colored poplin, glass buttons. Made in the one piece Empire style. The blouse has shaped revers, the skirt opens at front side. Value $400-450.

Afternoon 'frock' of white linen, piped in blue. The blouse is plain except for ornamental closing and embroidered collar. The sleeves are set in a plain way at the shoulders, and are cuffed at the elbow. The linen was heavy in this dress, the buttons of imitation lapis luzuli to match the piping. The four gore skirt is attached to the waist. Although this is a simple dress, it was considered fashionable and dressy. Value $400-450.

For afternoon wear linen was often preferred and in this dress the material is ramie linen; an imitation of real linen, but very soft and is half cotton. The waist is made in the Gibson style with a wide tuck extending over the shoulders and down the front and back of the waist. The closing is double breasted style the right side lapping well over the left. Flat turnover collar and in this model, still worn in 1913, the modified leg-o-mutton sleeve is evident. Seven gore skirt is joined at the waist. $375-400.

In 1913 the craze for Bulgarian embroidery was at its height, it was considered rich looking and effective. In a dress such as this which showed much attention to detail the owner was advised to wear it for several seasons. Pale blue linen with white trim embroidered in shades of blue and pink and white. The bodice has a yoke made without seams at the shoulder and quite shallow. Five gore skirt has a small inset panel showing embroidery which matches the yoke and cuffs as well as the belt. Value $500-550.

65

Fall, 1913. L. to R., Box coat, cut on raglan lines, worn with simple, tailored skirt. Coat, value $175-195. Walking dress; Plain blouse opens over a vest insert. Skirt is four gore. A walking dress was considered utilitarian, ideal for marketing, shopping or exercise. 1913. Value $325-375. Street dress to be worn without a coat. The dress has a coat-blouse effect with a 2 gore skirt. 1913. Value $350-375.

Suits from 1913. Three quarter length coat, 2 piece skirt. Sleeves have a little fullness at the shoulder. 2 piece skirt is plain at top and can be found in raised or regulation waistline. These suits are difficult to find. Value $350-400.

2nd from left: a semi-tailored calling gown, popular in Paris when something "plain" was called for. The coat which is cutaway in front discloses a vest, and has a little fullness at each side. Skirt has 3 gores. Value $350-400. For hard usage, including "business" this was the type preferred. The coat falls well below the hips and fastens below the waistline. 2 piece skirt absolutely plain. Value $350-400.

Ladies suits, 1915. This coat-suit boasts a jacket of the latest 1915 style. It extends over the hips, and has a front center closing. Revers and small collar, patch pockets, under the lap of these passes the narrow belt. Skirt is four gored and quite a bit of ankle showing is permitted with this style. Corduroy. $400-450. Ladies' dress. High standing collar, overblouse has yoke effect, skirt is circular cut which is closed in center front. Satin and net $450-500. Furs were often worn with this type garment, either around the neck or a muff as shown.

Black silk dress, sleeves are heavy with beads. Lace at neckline, beading at belt. This dress has a long train. Value $1,500-2000. Silk parasol $195-225.

1917-1918 maternity wear. In today's money these suits would cost $175 or more, so if found in good condition they are usually a bargain. For some reason maternity wear is found infrequently. Norfolk style suit with convertible collar, which is inlaid with silk velvet, fancy bone buttons, short skirt has full sweep with adjustable belt. Wool. Value $450-500.

1917-1918. All wool serge maternity suit. Loose lines held with adjustable belt, back slightly fitted to the waistline. Belt is trimmed with bone buttons and velvet. Large fancy collar trimmed with fold of velvet and buttons. Large patch pockets. Warmly interlined and lined. Skirt hangs in simple long line effect with inverted pleats at the front. Both of these have the self adjusting maternity waistband. The tailoring of these suits is so clever that pregnancy is well concealed. Large fur muff. Suit $450-500.

1918 Maternity wear, suits, each $450-500, if furred, $600-650. Hats $110-135. Notice the footwear.

1916 morning trousers $65-75. Jacket with tails, black, dated 1933 in pocket, $75-85; shown with Battenberg lace jabot from the 1920's, $45-55; 1930's black and rhinestone pin in jabot, $45-55. The outfit is displayed to emphasize the fact that it can be worn by a woman.

The rather plain jackets should range between $175 and $225. The wrap with its extra large armholes for the large sleeve is a very desirable item. Wraps of this type range between $500-750 again depending on materials, condition and trim.

Waist in the surplice effect, pretty much a rounded style. Tucks on both sides in front, button trim. The chemisette is removable because by 1910 the chemisette had displaced the guimpe. This waist is gray linen with soutache braid and linen buttons and was intended for the 'robust figure'. Value $200-250.

1906. Blouses of this type, depending on condition, fabric and detail range $250-350, hats of this year should cost between $150-200, again depending on material and trim.

70

Two blouses from the 1910-1911 period. This is a tucked blouse-waist which was considered rather plain for its time. Chiffon, round high collar. Closed at the back. This kind of blouse could easily be attached to a skirt to form a semi-princess gown. These blouses are much sought after for wearing today. Value $300-325.

Waist of embroidered Japanese crepe. Cluster of tucks at the shoulders give breadth to the shoulders. Standing collar. Value $300-325.

Left: The bodice of this waist is made over a French lining which is faced for the chemisette. The chemisette is in pointed outline. The waist is tucked in panel effect, closes left side of front. Wide tucks over each shoulder reach to waistline. Antique green satin waist, value $225-275.

Right: Gray cashmere waist with soutache trim joined to skirt of the same material. Chemisette is lace faced to a French lining and the bodice is cut in a rounded neckline. Waist value $225-275.

Left: White dotted swiss waist, simple and cool, round flat collar, thin silk, lined. For the most part waists were elaborate so these simpler types are great additions to a collection. Value $200-250. Right: Waist of the same period. Linen with lace insertions. High standing collar. Value depends on quality and amount of lace but in general all waists of this type should fall into the $200-450 range.

Left: 'Utility shirt waist' in a conservative styling, simply made and yet fashionable. Front has tucks, high standing collar and tie. It is made of filet net which is very difficult to find in good condition. Value $200-250. Right: Shirtwaist is of checked madras, another 'utility' good, everyday type waist. Value $175-200.

Although one piece dresses were becoming stylish blouses were still popular. This 1908 blouse is of satin messaline trimmed with ribbon roses, bowknots and lace. Also called a 'waist' the blouse was usually worn with the skirt of the same color and made of the same material in many cases. To be fashionable, at the very least the same color would have to be picked up somewhere on the skirt. Yoke is of tucked chiffon, reticella squares and a heavy applique form the motifs and scalloped effect. Exquisite. $350-450.

Handmade blouse, c. 1900. Four varieties of hand made lace, ¾ sleeves, tight wrists, handkerchief linen. $400-450.

A more efficient looking waist of tucked crepe de Chine with strips of Valenciennes lace set between the tucks. A fold of soft satin edged with little silk balls forms a deep square yoke effect and little straps of satin finish the outer edges of the sleeves. Value $295-325.

'Armistice Blouse.' Lightly gathered front with long collar falling softly over a center panel or 'vestee.' Made from a contemporary pattern by Folkwear. Value of original $135-150. Photo courtesy Folkwear, San Raphael.

1918 Blouse. The back of the blouse extends over the shoulders to meet the lightly gathered front and gathers at the back center waist into a self-tie or ribbon which encircles the waist to tie in front. Deep rectangular neckline. Made from contemporary pattern. Value of original, $135-150. Folkwear photo.

Jacket, c. 1900. Faille with passementerie and lace edged sleeves lined and neckline decorated with stemmed flowers and leaves. Value $350-400.

Above: short jacket, white silk with black applique, standing collar c. 1900. Value $300-350.

Right: Blouse - jacket, taffeta, blue, cream and black stripes, worn in 1900. Value $200-275.

Shirtwaists of this type should range between $200-400 depending on materials, workmanship and trim.

1905. All dresses and suits in this period and of these styles, unless they have some unusual features are priced at $350-550, but prices at this time vary from shop to shop and area to area. All prices on clothing of this period are rising very rapidly.

Left: This type garment is called a coat-suit and every woman was advised to have one in her wardrobe. The coat is a one-piece model with the seamless shoulder and a double breasted effect where the front closes. Belt across the front. Skirt is a four gore design closed at left side of back. Lower left side has tab extension where buttons are placed. Brocaded silk coat, plain silk skirt. Value $450-500. Right: Ladies' full length coat, soft cheviot, small collar and revers notched to form lapels. The sleeve is inserted without fullness at the shoulder and is cuffed. Satin trim. In 1912-1913 coats came in three lengths – full-length, seven-eighths length or three-quarter length. These are scarce. Value $500-600.

A stunning coat dress in light wool. An unusual burgundy color, it has a full length front panel of brocade. The gown has a long train and satin ribbon tie. Beautifully constructed gown. Value $600-750. Very early 1900's. Hat is straw with ostrich plumes, velvet and flowers. $145-175.

A fashionable Spring coat of 1910-1911. All the rage were the picturesque broad collars and flaring cuffs with unusual outlines. This is of satin in the Empire style. The coat has only two seams – under arm and shoulder and this gives the coat a graceful look and also only hints at the figure underneath. The collar is in contrasting satin braided in soutache and it nearly reaches the high waistline. The sash is attached to the coat. The sleeves have moderate fullness, cuffed in the same manner as the collar. This is not a typical style of the period and would be a tremendous find. Value $750-950.

Coat for very young lady. Matching skirt. Suit is of broadcloth with wide flaring cuffs of velvet with matching collar and pockets trimmed with velvet. Material trim on skirt is of contrasting color in broadcloth. Value of complete outfit $450-600.

Overblouse of linen, guimpe chiffon, skirt of linen with pleat and buttom trim on side. Belt is buckled. Value $450-500.

Figure on right in above photo is back view of suit on left.

Ecru light wool 'duster' coat with ornate braid trim. Lined in wool flannel. These are somewhat scarce and eagerly sought after by members of Vintage Automobile clubs. Value $350-450.

Coats for younger women. The style at left is known as 'Norfolk.' Made of serge, in a tailored design it has a velvet collar and is semi-fitted to accentuate the hipless, bustless ideal which was being emphasized in up-to-date coats of 1910 for this age group. The cutaway effect was also prominent, buttons still highly visible as trimming. The coat in the center is of broadcloth showing large buttons and button holes and velvet trim in a straight, loose fashion. Cutaway on right is made of herringbone suiting material, tailored in a princess style. Coats of this type, depending on material and trim are valued at $350-450.

Charles Stevens & Bros. advertisement, 1905. Coats of this kind, large sleeves and 50 inches long should range between $400-500. Hat on left, $75-125 in excellent condition. Hat on right, $75-125 in excellent condition.

Left to right: 1915. This dress has overtones of the shirtwaist, the extension of the sleeves forming a deep shoulder-yoke. The neck is soft and open with a flare collar. Two piece circular skirt which closes in the front. Oversized muff. Dress value $450-500. 1915. The coat is long waisted with double breasted closing, small roll collar. Wool with velvet trim. Coats are difficult to find especially with this interesting hemline. Value $375-500.

Ladies coats. These coats were worn over the skirts and waists and the general design is more or less the same. The differences lie in the way the coats were cut and how they are fastened. All have pockets and front fastenings and the cut determined whether the coat would have a round or square outline. Lapels on the two right coats are wide, the one on the left has narrow lapels. All are worn with elaborate hats. Coats of this type and quality without the matching skirt have a value of $400-425 depending on the trim. They can be found most often in broadcloth, cheviot or serge. If found with matching skirt value is $700-800. Almost all of these garments show magnificent tailoring.

Worth of Paris wedding dress. 1917. Silk illusion embroidered with genuine seed pearls in floral motif and trimmed with orange blossoms. Worth label.
Value $3,000-4,500.
Courtesy Museum of the City of New York

Betty Luther modeling beige sheer wedding dress, 1910 – at Gold Diggers' Fashion Show, Oct. 1977, Medford, Or. Kenn Knackstedt, photographer.
Courtesy: Southern Oregon Historical Society

Silk wedding dress. Gowns of this type and quality are almost timeless in their wearability and style. Extensive, magnificent bead work, draped sleeves, heavy silver thread used in the trim. Magnificent yet entirely comfortable to wear. Value $1,000-1,500.

Close up of bride and groom, 1912 wedding.

1912 wedding. Bride wears satin, lace and traditional veil with orange blossom headpiece and net train. Small ball fringe on dress yoke and sleeve edge. Chemisette of chiffon with high neck banded at top with small seed pearls. Dress, $850-1,000. Veil, $250-300. Bridesmaid, standing, satin dress, v-neck with lace insert, pearl and lace edging on cape. Dress, $650-750. Both wear long kid gloves, $40-55 pair. Boy wears linen jacket and pants (white) $100-125. Mens' suits, wool, value $150-225.

Wedding photo. 1903. Bride wears sheer voile, pleated bodice with lace yoke. High banded collar. Fullness and small cape at top of sleeves. Bride's dress had three ruffles and lace inset in skirt. Dress $1,500-2,000. Bridesmaid, left, sheer voile with ruffled skirt, large sleeve fullness and small cape effect at shoulder. Dress, $1,200-1,500. Mens' suits, with vests, wool, value, $175-225.

1913 house dress, wide collar on blouse, sleeve is cuffed at elbow. Three gore skirt opens in front over a small panel and is slightly gathered at the waist. This garment is without the small train whch was sometimes used at that time even in housedresses. The sash and little front panel is chiffon which was a new fancy in 1913. The cap is called a 'Charlotte Corday' cap and is made to match the dress. Figured cotton voile. These caps were adapted from the caps used by the servant class. Value of dress $275-325; cap $85-95.

Left: Japanese crepe kimono, satin trim, high shirred waistline, value $200-300.
Right: Tea gown of black China silk and net with satin trim. Both garments beautifully detailed and intended for informal wear at home. Tea gown value $400-600.

Kimono wrapper, shirred at the shoulders to fall in loose, straight folds to the hem. Sleeves are finished with a cuff and are flowing. Bands of plain material in green trim this kimono of lighter green dimity. Value of these kimonos is rising $150-175.

Tea gown or negligee. This is a lounging robe made of challis with shirring at waist. Value $250-275.

Morning wear. Left: one piece apron. Single piece, long seams at the sides, neck is a simple round, large arm holes. Usually found in calico or cambric or gingham. 1914. Value $30-40. Right: Ladies Kimono. Slender lines, panel front closing on its left side without fullness. Satin trim. 1914. Value $150-175.

1916. On left is a negligee gown. Plain sacque cut from shoulder to hem, apron front and back, hand scalloped trim. Found in various materials. Value $125-175. Maternity gown. Laced in front with darts which makes it adjustable. Skirt is one piece gathered at top with small frill. Found in various materials. Value $100-150. Combination corset-cover and short petticoat. Corset cover fastens in back. Short petticoat fits tightly. Lawn. Value corset cover, $55-75. Garment intact, $100-125. Petticoat, short, $55-75.

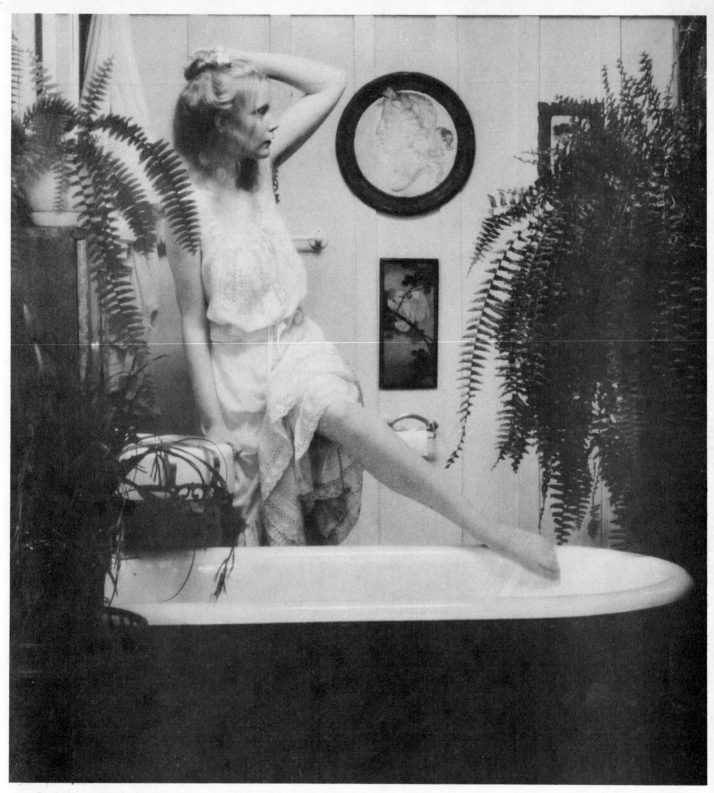

Camisole, c. 1900, the bodice of the camisole boasts tucks and lace inserts. Fitted in back, bloused in front, closes with drawstrings at neckline and waist. $95-115 value of original.
Photo courtesy FOLKWEAR, San Rafael, CA.
Gored petticoat has dust ruffle at hemline, drawstring waist ties at back. Value of original $100-200.
Knee length drawers gathered at the curved waistband, front gusset and 2 buttoned side plackets. Ruffles at knee. Value of original $125-155.

Bloomers attached to camisole top c. 1915-1919. Value $125-150.

Women's underthings: Left, c. 1915-1916 silk 'teddy.' A 'teddy is a camisole top and loose panties, combined in one garment. The 'teddy' shown is hand made and hand embroidered. Value $125-185.
Right: slip, c. 1920, hand embroidered. Value $75-95.

1914. Combination corset cover and drawers, embroidered with Irish crochet, value $195-250. The fine tucks at the waistline and at the edge of the drawers are hand-run. Batiste.

A combination garment of 1912-1913. 'Open drawers' and corset cover. Cotton. The slight fullness in front is regulated at the top by a ribbon running through the eyelet. The drawers are darted and fit snugly over the hips. This is hand embroidered but garments of this type can be lavishly trimmed with expensive laces. Depending on the trim the combination garment value is $125-200.

Tea gown or negligee. This is a lounging robe or 'demi-toilette'. Made of challis and worn with a fichu edged with ruffles of chiffon draped around the shoulders. Value $200-225.

Woman's undergarment, corset cover and drawers combined. Semi-princess style, made of cambric and ruffled. Value depends on trim but these are enjoying great popularity now. Value $185-250.

All clothing seems to have been categorized into time segments depending on function. This grouping presents 'morning wear' for all ages, a lady's dressing sacque and cap; lady's negligee, empire style; corset cover; apron which covers only front of the dress, the back is a deep yoke; boy's rompers cut in a single piece; child's dress with bloomers, simple sack shape; house dress of cotton. All of these are worthwhile additions to a collection and should be diligently sought after. Values follow general guidelines listed elsewhere in the book.

One of the important pointers to dating fashions is sleeves. Pictured here are sleeve styles of the 1906 period. These were considered by fashion writers of the day as "decidedly to the minute."

Bird body feathers swirl around red cherries on this Victorian hat. Black velvet with beading. 1890-1905. Value $150-175 Victorian collar, overall beading with black lace, value $65-100. Black ebony wood fan, black silk, black ribbon. End sticks covered with lace. Value $125-175. Black beaded bag, silver frame. Value $125-195.

These wonderful hats of the early Edwardian era are a revelation. They are decorated with flower-like rosettes of soft silk, often the whole hat or covering one side; they are made of fine or coarse straw, fancy braid and silk were used for the new Spring toques and turbans then coming into style again. The hats were becoming smaller in 1909 although by our standards they still seem oversized. Wings of feathers were often seen on hats of moderate size. Quilled ribbon is an indication of the age of these hats. The hair at this time was worn well over the brow and 'bangs' were having another revival. Value of hats depends on material and trim, as well as size in some cases, in good condition all should fall into the $200-300 range.

The truly magnificent hats of the years 1909-1910 are complementary to the equally impressive coiffeur of the ladies. Left hat features ribbons and full feather trim, right shows different kinds of feathers. Both are straw. Hats of this type are valued at $200-300.

Three different versions of the crocheted boudoir cap and different varieties of the hat stand.
Each cap $35-50.

1916. Boudoir cap of hairpin crochet, ribbon runs through loops and ties at the front. Value $35-50.

Boudoir caps in various styles and fabrics: satin, net, lace, ribbon and crochet work were the materials most used and many were made at home. Values clockwise, from center top: $45-55, c. 1900, $65-70; satin and crochet, $40-50; silk and lace $50-60; $35-40; silk and lace, $45-50.

Fans: various periods. Back feather ball fan, c. 1900 dyed lavender with matching bow and ribbon on handle. $65-75. Left: cardboard fan, ornate, with scenes on each panel, sentimental and among the most collectible of fans. $85-100. Center: child's fan, feather with pink rosettes. Difficult to find $75-85. Right: feather fan from China, pre-1920 wooden handle, Peking glass bead and enamel decoration $50-60.

Parasols, c. 1880-1910. Parasols have risen steeply in price. White lace with handmade black lace overall, value $275-300; beige silk and cerise silk in a hand-kerchief point design with a silk braided tassel on the wooden handle, value $200-225; child's black typically Victorian parasol, silk with ruffled edging, folding handle, value $195-225, high laced shoes in tan and brown leather.

Accessories: various periods. Combs resting on 1920's silk handkerchief. Backcomb set with small stones, c. 1908, $50-60. Side comb c. 1900, $35-40. Right: unusual tortoise shell comb set with rhinestone eagle $200-250. Umbrella handle, sterling silver. Cameos, all shell, all set in 14K gold: l to r: $325, $400, $165. Locket, gold filled set with brilliants, $65-95.

Part of a large beaded bag collection assembled over a relatively short period of time. The collector was paying about $55 to $175 for those shown. Most of those purchased within the last five years have doubled in price. The bags are hung from fancy hooks on a plain white wall to highlight their colors and shapes and designs. Any beaded bag collection (aside from its intrinsic worth and the delight of knowing one owns these treasures) can only be appreciated when displayed properly.

Fine French bags, all with chain handles. Left: French silk $100-155. Right: $95-125: Bottom: $200-225.

Selection of shoes from the early 1900's to 1920's. Black leather oxford, spool heel, ties, pointed toe, value $45-55; white canvas with spool heel. This type shoe was worn through the early 1920's and they seem to fit more people than other types, value $45-55; white leather, front lace $45-55; black leather, button strap, utilitarian wear of the 1920's, value $45-55. One problem with collectible shoes is the difficulty of finding a correct fit. Nevertheless shoes of bygone days in good condition are not easily found and should be purchased whenever they present themselves.

A selection of womens' shoes. Early 1900's white canvas hi tops, spool heel, cotton laces. Value $75-125; low cut black leather with beaded buckle, value $85-95; soft beige leather, lighter wool top, all lined, spool heel. For dress wear, value $175-195; low cut white canvas summer shoe, slip-on, bow of grosgrain ribbon, spool heel, hard rubber heel, value $85-100. Soft blue leather beaded 3 strap button shoe, spool heel. Value $100-135; silk lined heavy cotton shoe with spool heel, very pointed toe (partially hidden) burnt orange color. Value $100-125. Stuffing wadded tissue paper into the toes of these shoes can help them retain their shape.

Graduation dress of 1908. White, elaborately detailed with embroidered netting. Value $350-425.
Photo by Douglas R. Smith
Courtesy of Southern Oregon Historical Society

1914. Demure young high school graduate in the easy styling of lace and silk. Modest neckline. Very large corsage attached to belt. Value of dress $250-300.

Left: Suit for a young girl of 1909-1910. Reseda-green venetian, 2 piece semi-fitted coat which has cutaway effect, sleeve has moderate fullness but plain fitting sleeves were also popular. Turn back cuffs of velvet. Velvet faces collar. Seven gore skirt fits closely at hips and flares at lower edge. This is of serge and was the latest thing for the teenager in 1909. Value $325-400.

1908-1909. Center: Fitted dress, double row of front buttons, square neckline banded in velvet, buttons down sleeves which come to a point over the hands. Linen. Value $225-250.

Right: Teen-ager's dress or a dress for the 'young miss' of 1908-1909. White lawn with lace insertions, one of the most desirable types to collectors. Deep ruffle, tucks at bodice, moderately full sleeves gathered into armhole. Value $400-450.

Left: Dress for young miss. Simple design with fullness depending on the clusters of small tucks below the shaped yoke. The skirt is five gored with a large flounce. Linen with hand embroidery trimmed with bands of nainsook. It is often difficult to determine the age bracket into which some of the period clothing fits since size is not always a factor. Generally younger girls wore dresses of figured lawn, organdy or light weight woolens. The very small older woman has until recently had to go to these girlish styles. Value of dress $400-450.

Right: This young girl's gown was an exact copy of a dress intended for older women. It is semi-princess in sheath effect with a simple look. Slight fullness to the blouse-waist at the sides by single tucks at the shoulder, panel front and back are continued in the skirt which is joined to the blouse for the high waistline. Fancy neckline and short sleeves are provided for wear with a guimpe. This is old-rose cashmere. Value if material is in excellent condition $400-450.

1905 golfing and tennis costumes. The woman's outfit would probably be found as separates today and would fall into the price range quoted previously for 1900's blouses and skirts. This is also true of the gentleman's outfit, the pants would fall into the $40-50 range.

Misses' dresses, 1912. Left to right: Designed for the high school girl, this frock is rose cashmere. Middy style with sailor collar. Unusual lacing. Value $250-285. Middy dress, blouse is joined to a 6 gored skirt. Belt and sailor collar. Serge. Value $275-300. This dress closes at the left side of the front and has a 2 piece skirt. Cashmere, value $275-300. Lingerie dress. Embroidered flouncing with the yoke formed of rows of insertion with fine lawn. Organdy. Value $350-375.

Young ladies' wear is often sold as adult clothing even though it was shorter and the skirt was more boxy than the preferred ladies' gored type. Sizes were ordinarily 14 to 18 so again the waistline could have rivaled an adult waist. The look is different, much less fitted and looser. This sort of costume is very difficult to find, the range for the dresses would be $350-395 and the suits $400-500. The coats are again identifiable by the sleeve at the shoulder, and the rather high back strap. $250-275.

Gymnasium suits for young misses in 1913. Left, regulation type, plain blouse with round neck and small collar. Bloomers are separate and of moderate fullness. Lighweight flannel. Set value, $150-155. Blouse, $35-45. Bloomers, $75-85. Right: Same suit for the older girl, v-neck and pocket with striped sailor collar and sleeve edges. Value, set, $150-155. Blouse, $50-60. Bloomers, $75-85.

Winter of 1910. Young girl in typical clothing of the period, wool coat with low beltline and button trim with side closure. Large hat in the shape of a mob-cap with large feather wing trim. Coat value $200-250, hat $150-175.

1909. Young girl's dress of white pique with button-holed edges, box pleats from rounded neck to hem. Guimpe and one seam leg-o-mutton sleeves. Younger child's version has puffed sleeves. Older girl's dress is of tucked swiss, younger child's is of lawn. In either size, value $100-145.

A school dress of lawn trimmed with lace and embroidery. Fully lined. Small tucks in yoke effect. In a more elaborate material it could be considered a party dress. The shaped bertha gives the dress a certain elegance. Satin sash which bows in back. Large bows in hair. Value of dress $185-225.

1910. Young girl's cashmere dress trimmed with buttons. Front panel runs the entire length of the dress narrowing slightly from the neck to the waist then extending in a flare to the bottom of the skirt. Tucks over the shoulders back and front give fullness to the waist. Intended for a girl up to 14 years of age. This is pique. Value $200-250.

1910. White linen with embroidered bands. Dress closes at left front with 2 wide tucks over shoulders to waistline in front. Puff sleeves which were favored for younger girls up to about 9. Value $195-250.

For a girl up to 14 or 15 this navy blue repp dress was considered very fashionable in 1910. Buttons down side for trim, tucks extend into skirt, dutch collar, belted. Value $195-250. Large hair bows much in evidence.

Left: A 1909 boy's suit in the Russian style. Regulation knickerbockers attached to waist bands. The blouse has a wide sailor collar and a removable shield. The sleeves are gathered very slightly into the armhole and finished at the wrist with a band. There is a single pocket left front. Belted. Flannel. Boys suits of this era are among the most difficult clothing to find. Value $295-325.

Center: Little girls' dress of lawn. Considered a play dress or a party dress entirely dependent on the material and trim. Collectors of children's clothing need to be aware of the factors which separated the categories in this kind of clothing. Clusters here of tucks stitched from the neck and shoulders to yoke depth. This dress has a dutch round neck and short puff sleeves. Insertions of beading and ribbons at neck, sleeves and belt. $200-250.

Right: 1909 girl's dress intended for a child up to 8 or 9 years of age. Dotted swiss with high neck and long sleeves, tucked, green satin sash. Value $200-250.

Young girl of the early 1900's. Long wool, high waisted dress with hem ruffle. Emphasis on shoulder and sleeves which are long with puffed oversleeve, with an overall cape effect. Necklace and bar pin. Not much more clothing could possibly adorn such a small person. Dresses of this kind are scarce. Value $250-350.

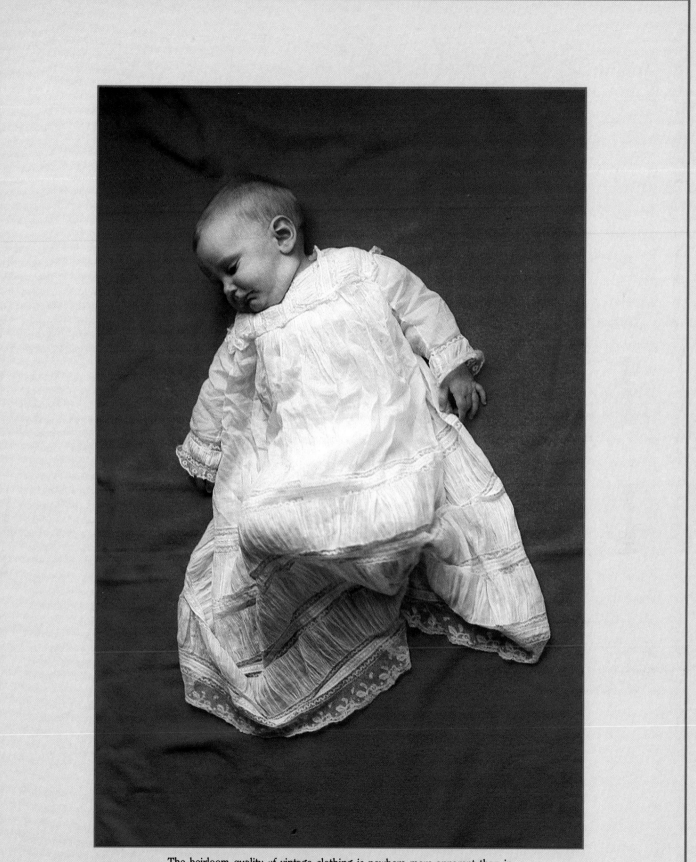

The heirloom quality of vintage clothing is nowhere more apparent than in
the christening gowns of bygone days. This long christening robe was first worn in 1879 by the grandfather
of the infant pictured. It is cotton lawn with hand made lace. Victorian christening gowns are in such demand
a British company makes them to order to exacting old standards guaranteed to fool everyone. The company
which specialized in these garments charges $80-110. Originals command higher prices if they can be found.
The beautifully made dress this baby wears is valued at $200-250

Lavender silk dress with overskirt. Off-white dots. Permanent pleats in skirt, chiffon sleeves. Neckpiece ties in back in a low V. This is a gorgeous dress. Value $450-500

Blue silk-satin dress with gold thread design. Silk chiffon sleeves. Lace collar. Value $400-500. Straw hat, black with blue ostrich feather and decorative pin. Value $85-100

Blue lingerie dress with lace inserts. Bands of embroidery and lace inserts also on sleeves and on skirt. Sewn down pleats on skirt flare out, buttons down back. Value $400-475

Black silk 1930's dress with pleated white silk collar. Bottom cut on the bias. Value $300-350. Black straw hat with large gold and black velvet flowers. $45-50

Peach silk crepe 1940's dress. Draped neckline, horizontally pleated skirt caught up in a side drape. Value $100-145. Open toe suede pump, needlepoint handbag with celluloid handle $25-35

Wedding dress and veil first worn in 1935. Lace dress over silk slip. High ruffle at neck is fine net. Veil is net with a lace cap trimmed with orange blossoms. Dress and veil worn here at a 50th anniversary party in 1985 by the bride herself. It is very difficult to assess the worth of these gowns since sentiment is often the overriding interest. Excellent workmanship, fabric and condition are important. 1930's wedding dresses are becoming more valuable as collectors realize their style and quality. Value $450-650

Wool gabardine taupe suit with padded shoulders. Suits were an absolute necessity to the well-dressed woman's wardrobe in the 1940's. This has a notched collar and closes at the waist with two buttons. Peplum flare to jacket. These suits can be very flattering to the figure. Value $125-145. The hat is wool tweed with brown feather $25-30; shoes are alligator with bow $45-50; handbag is also alligator $50-75. Kid gloves. The scarf of stone-martens are valued at $250-300

Late 1950's double knit two piece dress. These are very abundant and would be an easy, interesting way to begin a clothing collection. Value $25-45. They are undervalued. Mink Stole value $125-175

Light lavender chiffon beaded dress with pearls around hemline. 1920's. Value $600-750

This brown velvet blouse has a detachable collar which is attached by hook and eye. 1880. The blouse measures 18″ around the waist. Value $250-275. The hat is black velvet with gold ostrich feathers, hand tied to give extra strength. Value $100-150

Selection of beaded bags. The two smaller bags are child size and were made specially for the author in 1938 when this was a popular, if somewhat tedious craft. The red and black were also made to order for family members but are somewhat earlier in the 1930's. All beaded bags are highly collectible and there are truly spectacular collections of such bags extant. Values of beaded bags vary greatly. Any good beaded bag should have a minimal value of $55, many reach into the several hundreds of dollars.

Off-white crepe dress of the 1940's. Draped front with beading. Mandarin neckline, mid-calf length. $125-150

Selection of fans, not only a favorite fashion accessory but the favorite of multitudes of fan collectors. 1880's white feather fan, 1920's blue and gilt oriental fan with beaded handle, child's feather fan with French rosettes on the tip of each feather, and a pink Ball fan of the 1880's early 1900's.

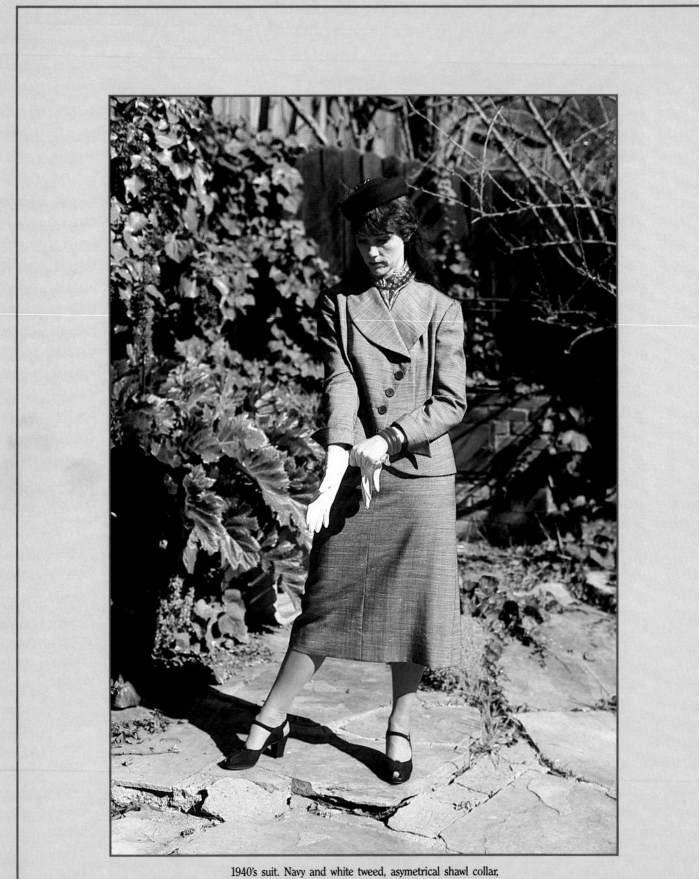

1940's suit. Navy and white tweed, asymetrical shawl collar,
¾ length sleeve. Value $125-135. Necklace, matching bracelet and earrings are of red celluloid. Shoes are black suede with small platforms, ankle strap closing $25-35; hat is small felt suit hat $20-22

1908 Child's playwear or play suit. Two wide tucks at the shoulder in front and an inverted plait at the back below the waistline afford fullness. This fastens down front left and has a standing collar. Bloomers are optional. This is of percale and intended for a little girl up to 10 years of age. These are often quite beautiful and are scarce. Value $200-300.

Party frock for the very young girl of the 1908-1910 period. Yoke of embroidery, high neck, full length sleeves. This is of batiste. Children's clothing continues to be popular. $135-185.

Same basic dress with added sash and different neckline. For older child. Girls wear shoes with straps and bows. Value of dress $195-225.

Left: 1909 Wrap intended for young girl. Cold or rainy day covering. It is basically a 4 piece cape which fits smoothly about the neck and shoulders and widens below the hips. Rolling collar. Fastens in front with opening for hands. Waterproof serge which lends itself perfectly to this military style. Scarce. Value $275-300. Sometimes found with a hood.

Box coat for little girl, also worn by older girls. Wide square collar with braid effect which is repeated on sleeves. Broadcloth. Shown as worn by both ages. Value $195-250. These young girls are wearing the huge hats decreed as fashionable by their mothers but seem overwhelming on the children.

1913. Junior styles. Favorite yoke model dress in a plain sacque design which hangs straight from the shoulder to the hem and applied on this is the novel yoke which comes down almost to the waistline. Wide collar and cut off sleeves. Hand scalloping on edge of collar and sleeves. Linen. Quality of the material and handwork add greatly to the value of garments such as these. Value $185-225.

This apron resembles a dress. It is a coverall type which completely covers the dress beneath. It is a Mother Hubbard or Kate Greenaway style made with a yoke which extends well down on the chest and back. Full skirt, high neck with turnover collar. These were always made in washable fabrics. Cambric. Value $95-125.

Two piece dress, the skirt being attached to the underwaist which fasten in back. V neck. The blouse coat has a diagonal closing in front and a broad band in Balkan style at the lower edge. Poplin. $185-200. 1912.

1913. For school or play. The large bow at front waist line distinguishes this dress. Gingham. $95-115. This dress is for the very young child. There is more interest at the moment in clothing for younger children. This affects prices. Wide box pleat down the front and back wide collar. Belted. Value $100-115. Sacque cut, front cut with deep U and filled in with a laced chemisette with collar. Cashmere. Value $150-175.

Child's sweater, cap and muff set of ostrich wool. Sweater and muff have cross stitching design, muff is satin lined. Cap has large satin ribbon bows. Worn over white linen cambric dress. Stockings are long and worn with high button shoes. Value of sweater, muff and hat as a set $200-250.

Top, girls' coat, high neck, small collar, circular skirt. Wool. Value $150-175. Left, made of different materials which was considered 'new' in 1916. Serge top with velvet skirt. Value $145-165. Separate skirt and blouse, which is long length. Satin with wool. Value $135-155.

Boy's Russian suit. This easy to launder suit has a front closing blouse. Made of chambray, these are endearing additions to a collection. Value $125-155. An 'Oliver Twist' suit which consists of shirt waist with pleats and straight trousers buttoning to the shirtwaist. Value of suit $125-145.
Girl's dress of 1914. A child's kimono dress slips over the head. Drawers are worn under the dress. Cotton. Value $55-65.
Teenaged girl's short jacket of plaid wool worn with plain colored wool skirt. Jacket $85-125. Notice large tam and high shoes.

1909 girl's reefer. Gray broadcloth, notched collar, cuffs and pockets finished with stitching. Close fitting sleeves with gathers at top. Worn by girls up to 14. Value $120-240.

Right: same coat intended for younger child. Value same. Notice overwhelming hats on young children.

Center. 1909. Child's coat in the Empire style, following the adult fashion. Wide fancy collar and cuffs. Blue bengaline silk. $150-200. Button shoes.

Body and sleeves of this coat are one piece. Belted. Wool. Value $95-115. Girls' dress. Copied from a new fashion for women in the winter of 1913, the deep, straight yoke. A row of shirring at the waist, and over this a wide belt. Plaid silk with velvet trim. Value $125-150. School dress for winter. Serge, value $95-115.

Summer frocks, 1913. Diagonal front closing, wide shawl collar ending at belt which has buttons below, linen. Value $145-175. Seamless shoulder in drop style, ribbon threaded through for effect, cotton. Value $100-145. Bodice and skirt dress. Simple style with wide banding trim. Skirt joins waist beneath belt, cambric. Value $100-125.

Boy's single breasted overcoat. Well fitting collar and rolled lapels. Usually found in wool. 1913. $100-125.

1915. Girls' apron. One piece with a short dart below arm to adjust to figure. Closes in back. Gingham. $30-40. Girls' coat. Simple box type, raglan sleeves. Tweed. Value $95-120. Boy's overcoat, with long shoulder-cape which does not cover coat buttons in front. Detachable cape. Wool. Value with cape $150-175. Coat without cape, $95-125. Cap in child's size, $25-35.

For the small child, 1915. Top left: Garment is quite simple, front side closing. Square neck, can be worn by boy or girl. Serge but can be found in velveteen. Value, $95-135. Boy's Russian dress. Wool, high neck with banded collar, closing well over to side in front. $95-150. Simple dress with plain blouse with drop shoulder and wide collar. Diagonal closing across front and meets line of skirt closing. Value $100-145. Boy's suit. Coat of modified Eton type, edges meet at neck but hang apart to hem of jacket which ends below the hips. Vest and trousers made without a fly. Velveteen. Value $200-250. Slip type dress with guimpe. Small box pleats front and back. Dress with belt $95-125.

1915. Sacque cut, shirring at neck and waist for children up to 6 years of age. Challis. Value $95-125. Long waisted blouse with pleated skirt. Collars and cuffs match hem border. Belt. Value $100-125. Tunic over waist and skirt. Belt of leather at low waistline. Tunics were also popular with the ladies of 1915. Value $110-145. Sailor dress with collar which joins revers with notches. Pleated skirt. Cashmere. $135-165.

1915. Children's coat. Plain sacque coat with highly ornamental cape. Round neck is trimmed with a small collar and the full sleeves end in a cuff. Value $150-175. Often these children's coats were made in expensive materials such as ottoman silk, velvet, cashmere, fur. The bonnet, which went with this kind of coat was also usually silk or velvet, is round and full, finished with a flat band around the head. Value $45-55.

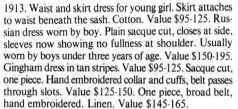

1913. Waist and skirt dress for young girl. Skirt attaches to waist beneath the sash. Cotton. Value $95-125. Russian dress worn by boy. Plain sacque cut, closes at side, sleeves now showing no fullness at shoulder. Usually worn by boys under three years of age. Value $150-195. Gingham dress in tan stripes. Value $95-125. Sacque cut, one piece. Hand embroidered collar and cuffs, belt passes through slots. Value $125-150. One piece, broad belt, hand embroidered. Linen. Value $145-165.

1913. Dresses for the small girl. Long bloused effect, pleated skirt, bow at neck, button front. Cotton. Value $95-125. One piece dress with attached bloomers. Green challis with rosette of blue satin at side. Value $95-125. One piece with front closing and separate guimpe. Value $100-135. School coat. Box style, circular front, contrasting trim. Value $135-145. Utility dress made in many washable materials as well as wool. Value $95-125. Embroidered flouncing on this one piece dress. Closes at back. Value $135-165. Large bows if original, $30-40.

In 1912 boys hats were fashionable when they were 'shapeless' and made of cloth. In typical style the crown fits over the head and the brim is stiffened by means of stitching. The jockey cap was also a favorite and is now making a minor comeback especially among girls. The cap with visor is flannel. Notice the variety of ties worn with the same collar. Value of boys hats of this kind and era $25-45.

C. 1916. Cotton with lace dress. $95-125.

1912. Baby's short dress in crochet. The flounce and upper part of the skirt was made separately and attached to the waist. Surprisingly durable for all its fragile look. This beautiful handwork is now eagerly sought after and a dress combining this beauty and marvelous crochet work would be of heirloom status if found in excellent condition.
$300-325.

Boy's suit, blue serge, paneled front, 2 piece. Bow of linen. C. 1900. Value $135-165.

Child of the 1920's. Knitted suit with straps to hold pants over shoes, matching cap. Small sized icecream chair. Value of suit $95-145.

Long cambric infant's baptismal dress, worn first by boy, 1900, handmade, standing collar. Worn again recently. Value $165-195.

Baby bonnets are still inexpensive, often beautifully made with extravagent fabrics and trim and are still relatively easy to find. A truly wonderful rewarding collection could be made of these. Left is pink crepe with hand embroidery $25-30; pink silk with ruching and lace, value $40-45; Irish lace with pink silk lining $45-55; linen bib with white embroidery $20-25 (bibs are another underappreciated collectible); long linen bib with lace trim. $45-55.

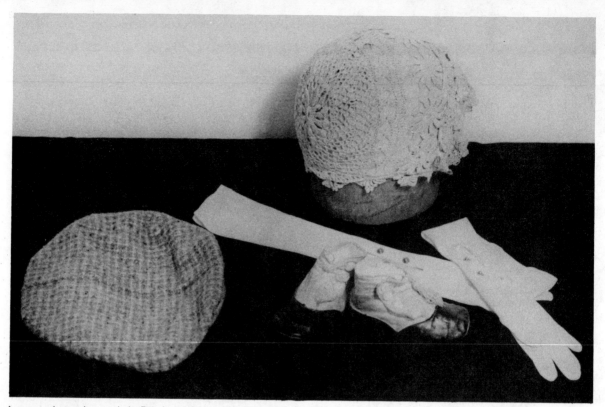

Children's accessories: various periods. Baby's cap, handmade, lined with silk, c. 1917, $40-50. Boy's woolen cap, c. 1930, value $22-25. Shoes, patent leather and kid, buttons and tassels, 1914. Value (worn condition) $20-25. Young girl's long gloves, silk and rayon, $18-22.

A baby saque or sack in material which could be laundered. This is of French flannel embroidered in silks with scallops forming the edges. Value $45-55. Another sack with a turn-over collar and scalloped edges. Crepe de chine but these are often found in linen or cashmere. Value $45-55.

The reason vintage baby clothes are so beautiful and expensive is the attitude toward their making, "all infants garments should be of the softest, finest materials, made by hand and never trimmed with coarse, cheap lace." These bonnets are hand made and embroidered. On left is a bonnet with wide strings and made of lawn; center is a hat made of corded silk with a 12 inch diameter; another bonnet embroidered and ribbon run through the soft linen. Value of baby bonnets and hats of this quality $45-65.

This baby clothing is most often found in nainsook, poplin, pique or soft linen. Dress is stamped Irish poplin. It was intended to be worn over a guimpe. Irish poplin is a lustrous mercerized cotton of good wearing quality. Embroidered. Value $45-60.

# MAID UNIFORMS

What the Maids were wearing in 1916. This costume was called the 'La Mode' and was considered the 'service dress de luxe'. Black cotton pongee with white trim. Scarce. Value of dress, apron and cap $200-250.

Another of the LaMode line. This is of white cotton pongee. 1916. Value $250-275. Ankle length.

Sampling of clothing label collection. More common types $1-2. Designer type $5-10.

Another man's suit of 1910, wool and tailor made to specific measurements. Value $200-250. At this time suits 'off the rack' were becoming more available to men.

The well-dressed man of 1910, replete with pipe and bulldog. His striped wool suit with cuffed pants and very large buttons has wide revers. Suit with vest $200-250.

College graduating class, 1905. Woman's dress, $400-425. Gentlemen wear the high buttoned frock coat, vests with high rounded collars and importantly placed buttons, one wears striped trousers, notice the differing ties. Complete suits, $500-550.

Dandy of 1912, striped trousers, long jacket, pearl button vest, small, rounded collar. Vest, $95-110. Jacket $110-145. Trousers $55-100.

Couple of 1905. She wears a wool dress with lace chemisette and trim. His 3 piece wool suit is formalized by the collar and tie. Value of dress $400-500, man's suit $250-350.

This gentleman of 1911 obviously opted for comfort with his soft collar. His wide tie features a lovely, rather large, square cameo tie pin. His wool coat is bound in satin and the fancy buttons are self-covered. Value of tie pin $150-200; value of coat $200-250.

Formal wear of the early 1900's. Black cashmere, satin trim on lapels, jacket and sleeves. Vest has matching trim. Black and gray striped trousers with original suspenders. Coat labeled: Von Longerde & Antoine, Chicago, Ill. Value $300-400. There is a great demand for mens' clothing of this type. Gray top hat and a watch fob which is a family piece.

The lady wears a raw silk duster trimmed in black satin embroidered with gold thread and sporting large gold buttons. Value $450-550. Straw hat trimmed with pink flowers and worn with a green hat scarf. Value $150-175. The gentleman wears white wool striped trousers with a red and white striped shirt, brown and white tie with a brown wool jacket and a straw boater. The automobile worthy of all this wonderfully collectible clothing is a 1914 Cole 5 passenger touring car.

The dress is of white cotton batiste with two tiered skirt. Heavy embroidery on waist and sleeves. Value $350-450. White canvas high-top shoes. The hat is straw covered with horsehair net and decorated with small velvet flowers. Value $145-165.
The gentleman wears gray wool trousers with a gray and white seersucker jacket, a white driving cap and black shoes.

Full dress suit of 1901. Watch fob prominent. High collar, vest. Fobs are now widely collected and valued according to material and stones. Full dress suit in excellent condition $400-500.

Business suit of 1901. Rounded effect, high collar, derby hat and prominent watch fob, all fashionable in the early 1900's. These suits are very difficult to find. Value $275-300. Derby hat $45-55

'Outing suit' intended for a day at the shore or similar activity. Contrasting jacket and trousers. Almost impossible to find as a set. 'Boater' hat of straw $50-65.

118

Mens' shoes of the early 1900's. Black leather with felt top with buttons. Value $75-100; black leather oxford with tie laces $35-45; black leather with felt top and buttons, 'pull tab' showing. Value $75-95.

Man's cotton starched collar, white, c. 1900, $10-15; black neck scarf, knitted, one front snap closure at neck, value $20-25; white knitted man's scarf similar to the black, one front neck snap closure. These were worn under a coat to provide warmth in the popular touring cars. Value $20-25. Mens' socks, silk, 1930's $10-15; garters for silk socks which did not have elastic tops, 1930's $15-20; mens' ties, painted silk, 'tie yourself' $5-10. Crafts people are buying these for many other uses other than clothing collections. At top are mens' ties which were pre-shaped to fit $5-15.

The well dressed man of 1916-1917. Tie pin, stiff collar, cuff links and well brushed hair. The strong-jawed look promoted by Charles Dana Gibson. Value of these collars is $12-15, even more collectible is the delightful collar boxes which held them

# CHAPTER III

# 1920-1940

No wonder we are dazzled by the 1920's. A time in the United States when triumphant post war fever swept the land, it was a time to release tension, a time to let go. Americans were having the last big fling, although they didn't know it. There was more freedom for women and the entire attitude was young. Women bobbed their hair, did the frenzied Charleston and listened to jazz. The evening clothes reflected the outlook, it was easy, it sparkled and it was a trifle bizarre.

The flapper leaped out of every page. Mention the word today and a vision of pencil thin, bobbed haired beauty, wearing her rather shapeless beaded dress and long colored beads comes instantly to mind. She also wore cloche hats, although later in the decade hats became large and lovely, and her waistline was only suggested by bands near the hip line. In truth many of the dresses of this period can be found in rather large sizes so not everyone was petite. The style was generally flattering to the figure, being basically straight line and loose.

The hair and the hats were prominent fashion features in the 20's. The cloche was it. Tightly moulded to the head, sometimes with a narrow brim, it was worn well down on the forehead. It was made of felt, silk, velvet, satin or crepe and it complemented the dresses beautifully. The individual touches on the hats were enchanting — "a brilliant pin placed on the right front side", or "a peaked cloche of capuchine crepe satin trimmed with long feathered bands which break into soft tufts at the apex".

"Millinery", said a prominent 1920's magazine, "is not just making hats, no indeed. Millinery in its creation is an art." It was, and is, true that the proper headpiece considers facial contours, skin and hair coloring, and the coiffure will frame the face in a flattering way. Also the proper hat can strike a master stroke for individuality. Coordinated properly with the dress or suit it is that last finishing touch.

Plain silk frocks decorated with colored silk flowers, or 3 sprays of silk roses with silver encrusted leaves and flexible stems on a rustling taffeta dress might match the spray of flowers on the hat. The flowers on the hats were made of silk or chiffon or sheer gauze. The lapel flower made an appearance at this time and has never entirely deserted the fashion scene since.

The cloche hat survived into the 1930's but it did not continue to dominate the 20's scene; by 1926 large brims were the rage. But time was running out on the hat industry. During the early 20's many thousands were employed in the hat industry in New York alone. What has happened to all those hats and elegant headgear of the 1920's? It seems to be one of the most difficult of periods from which to find good representative millinery but when such a piece is found it is usually a gem.

The beading on the evening dresses make these garments the goal of every 1920's vintage clothing collector, and often are sought by collectors of clothing of other periods. Not only is the workmanship superb, the beads glittering and worked into intricate designs, but the dresses are still eminently wearable if found in good condition.

Some are so heavily beaded that care must be taken in their display. Hangers are unsuitable and if a dress form is not available, the dress should be folded and stored carefully. Ready-made beaded panels could be bought separately and added to the basic slip-like dress.

Today, long after the heyday of these glamorous gowns, any collector of vintage fashion would be delighted to add one to a collection, and even non-collectors covet them. Today, everyone seems to love this fashion.

Displayed on a dress form the dresses seem to have a life of their own, they shimmer and change colors in different light and aside from their obvious beauty this may also be part of their appeal. The satins and chiffons move with every breeze. Sequins were also used generously in the late 20's as the curved and pointed irregular hemlines began to inch downward. Waist lines were still low on the hips, long dangling earrings were clearly visible with the short hair, and in evening wear the keynote was a kind of casual elegance.

In fact fashion arbiters were advising 'the studied, careless look'. "Avoid a dressy look, even in formal clothes," they said, and had some words of wisdom for the young college miss. "The college girl should wear felt hats, dented here and there nonchalantly, soft, pull-on gloves sufficiently large to crush generously, plain sandals or pumps, and all of this will create the well groomed but studied careless air that in this year of 1924 is really chic." Today's college girl would swoon at the thought, but when you find a 20's look hat that is dented here and there, it is more likely by design than accident.

Suits with matching frocks and a ¾ matching coat were fine for street wear or a ¾ length blouse of material to match the coat and worn with a tight skirt, was considered more than acceptable and the slightly mannish look of the earlier 20's was passing. The ensemble idea was stressed and capes were being worn again. Masculine type lounging robes were being worn by women and wide leather belts worn low on the hips were the big accessories.

The beaded bags which these lovelies carried already have so many devotees, it is probably sufficient to remark on their workmanship and beauty. It is rather late to begin such a collection because prices have risen steeply and continue upward. Already there exist many large collections of these, but if beaded bags are your fancy they are a beautiful investment.

The young people who danced all night in their fancy satin shoes were lively to the point of exhaustion. Our essential national innocence had been dissipated by the 'war to end all wars' and in the 20's the accent was on youth, 'flaming youth'. The flapper became a by-word.

John Held Jr. created her and named her 'flapper', so the story goes, because she often wore galoshes with the buckles undone and they flapped as she walked. Whatever the exact origin of the word, its two small syllables sum up an entire era.

Until recently the rental companies dealing in vintage clothing had few flapper types to loan. Not too long ago a college student friend sought in vain for a beaded dress, proper shoes and a feathered headband to wear to a school dance. Finally she borrowed the dress seen on page 151 (center) from a private collector. It was such a success and elicited so many inquires the collector now rents her clothing to selected customers. Business is brisk. She feels that she is educating the public, many of whom have never seen such clothing, especially the young people. Anyone with a good vintage clothing collection should definitely share it in some way with others, club meetings, junior groups of young people, convalescent homes, even schools. That is the ultimate joy of collecting; the sharing.

The girlish look of the early 1920's, reinforced by the soft materials used in the dresses, contrasted sharply with some of the movie stars of the day, personified by Pola Negri and her 'vamp' image. Other Hollywood stars held out against bobbing their hair, but the late Gloria Swanson was an early convert. This indecision about image was reflected in hem lengths which varied from knee length to calf length to almost ankle length.

Coco Chanel came along with her classic look that still retains a measure of popularity, and it is felt that in her the 20's spawned one of the great dress designers.

The short dresses of the early 20's led to more interest in the shoe. The Louis heeled, long pointed vamp, and T-strap pumps were entirely visible beneath the uneven hemlines of points or fringe.

For collectors shoes can show some wear if it does not affect the material of the uppers. Perfection is always the goal, but in the search for shoes this becomes very difficult. Proof of the fact that even some party clothes were worn often by the average person is the wear often found on the shoes of the 1920's. The shoes are intriguing though, and anyone collecting in the period needs at least one or two pairs to delineate the dress.

The shoe buckles are even more fun. Four years ago cut steel buckles could be bought for $4 or $5, and two years ago I paid $8 to $12 a pair. Recently prices have moved into the $30-$40 range. Although I have seen collections of buckles which are singles, it is wiser to search out the pairs. The values will hold and of course, it's necessary if they are to be worn unless you are a real trend setter and are willing to wear a different buckle on each shoe.

Although the cut steel are usually fine quality the rhinestone sets can be spectacular, but are somewhat more difficult to find. Often the backings are made of velvet, or satin, or patent leather, although some were made without any backing at all.

Shoe buckles can be traced to the Celts (600 B.C.) and since those ancient days their popularity has waxed and waned but never completely disappeared. There is tremendous variety in shoe buckles and their charm is a decided asset to a clothing collection. Recently at auction a pair of cut steel buckles in their original box sold for $75. We collectors are certainly on the right track.

And just what is happening in the auction market? Some larger auction houses are holding sales geared only to vintage clothing and interest is always high.

Furs seems to hold a special appeal for collectors who buy them not only to display but to wear. Recently a full length ocelet coat with a narrow mink trim sold for $4,000 at auction. This is a tremendous rise over a similar coat on which I had bid about 4 years ago.

Furs must be previewed very carefully since the small splits which develop as the fur dries out cannot always be noticed in a casual perusal.

The reason for this clamor for vintage furs is three-fold: 1. Their usefulness, 2. their scarcity, not only as vintage clothing but because many animals which were used to make those furs are now on endangered species lists and so the fur piece can never be duplicated. 3. luxury, the feeling that wearing an elegant fur coat imparts cannot be explained fully, but if you've never worn a vintage fur, try it, you'll like it. Another consideration is that the older fur coats are unusual bargains, often times many hundreds of dollars less expensive than they were originally.

The velvet shown on page 144 is a perfect example. Where today could a coat of such quality and beauty be bought for the price quoted, where today could one buy a coat with such style and flair? Made in the 1920s it is flattering to the figure, the color is exquisite and anyone lucky enough to own it could hardly avoid a feeling of glamour. Isadora Duncan may or may not have worn it, but it certainly brings her to life.

The vintage clothing collector of the 1920's period should follow the general advice of dating within a decade unless historical research demands pinpointing. However, quite specific changes makes some years easily definable.

1920 women wore deeply crowned hats, the skirt was at ankle length or a bit shorter, the beltline was at the hip, long sleeves were tight and wrist length. The exposed leg cried out for slinky silk stockings and the beaded necklace became almost a badge.

In 1923-24 the cloche hat vied with the large organza or 'garden party' type, dresses were mid-calf length and rising, shoes had the Louis heels which were used thoughout the 20's and the shoes themselves could be made of satin, kid or leather. The hip belt was still in fashion.

1925-1926. The big news was the hemline, now knee length. Women wore bust flatteners and girdles and fancy underwear. Petticoats or slips in beautifully detailed silk with narrow shoulder straps and lace and embroidered trim. These were worn short, well above the knee. It is mostly these slips and petticoats and the silk lounging pajamas which entice collectors today. The materials are fine, the workmanship exquisite and some are so elegant that they can be used today. At a recent party in New York a guest was wearing heavy silk lavender lounging pajamas under a silver fox jacket. The costume created a minor sensation. The undergarments should be a highly specialized collecting area. There are enough of them available to build a good collection without too much effort and they require less care than the gowns.

A minor revolution occured in the 1927-1929 period. The V-neckline was introduced and created controversy. The T strap shoe and cloche hat were still worn and generally there was a crossover of all styles.

By the 1920's it should be remembered that the made-to-order clothing catalogues were advertising ready to wear outfits for one and all. Now people could look beyond their Sunday best or 'company' outfit and indulge themselves with full wardrobes without too much expense and bother. This applied to the clothing of men and children as well as women. A large variety of styles and types were offered and the choices offered are reflected in the many 1920's garments we can now choose from.

Although all periods are reflected by the way people dress, the clothing of the 1920's is perhaps one of the most precise indicators of its time. It was an exciting decade, it had an air of forbidden fruit about it, it was a time of great changes and as the decade moved to its frantic close, economic barometers were predicting disaster.

If you are already a collector, or thinking of collecting clothes from the 20's try for a reputable dealer who handles only the best quality. Such a person will assure that your dress' beadwork is intact, the clothing clean, the hats have their original trim, appropriate shoes, and the furs soft and wearable; all the things that are important to the definitive collector who wishes to build a valuable, in depth collection.

Everybody today thinks back on the 1920's as a riotous time. For some, it surely was, but the millions who wore the ordinary clothing of the day are being neglected, their dresses and suits are interesting too. But everybody wants those beads.

Men of the 1920's were still in a conservative mood. The wide trousers were a change, sometimes they were as much as 22 to 24 inches at the bottom. Knickers or plus fours were big with sportsmen and were buckled four inches below the knee, hence the name 'plus fours'.

Lighter colors were favored in summer but cold weather called for another of those items which makes an age memorable — the raccoon coat. All the college boys had them and some of the co-eds too. I inherited a raccoon coat in perfect condition and wore it in the 1950's. Recently I saw a young man in San Francisco sporting just such a coat. It was like a one man fashion show. The raccoon coat, a great coat in every sense of the word, useful, stylish even now, and large, larger even than life.

That was the 1920's....

If the 1920's prove one half of the adage that hemlines go up when the stock market goes up, the 1930's surely prove the other half, the hemlines go down when the stock market drops. By 1930 skirts were longer, and the waistline was again in its normal place, nothing else seemed normal though.

When historians refer to the 30's, we read about "the great depression", the songwriters were asking, "Brother can you Spare a Dime", but fashion dictators were advising longer hair, wider shoulders, narrow hips and in evening new emphasis on the back.

Many Americans can recall the time with great clarity. As children, the depression shaped their futures in all ways, and encouraged a sense of caution. Many, left with a sense of thrift born in those difficult days, never discarded the clothing of that period and so collectors today have an opportunity not always possible when dealing with other times; except for Art Deco fans, not too many collectors have taken advantage of the opportunity.

For years clothing of the period was neglected. People who had lived through the bleak years did not want to be reminded and the young had not yet begun to consider the rather shapeless day wear attractive. But as we continue to be more removed in time from the 30's we can focus on what was good rather than bad and can decide what a good collection should include.

The best of the clothing and the evening wear is only now attracting buyers in numbers. At no time, for example, has there been a more simple but classic design than the plain black velvet evening dress of the 30's. It is so characteristic that collectors simply refer to it as "the thirties black velvet". It is stark and beautiful, can be worn unadorned or with ornamentation equally well. That, in fact, may be a summation of the 30's fashion scene.

America's dress image became blurred — factories were manufacturing clothing by the ton — and anybody who could afford it could wear any clothes that appealed. This was the early period of homogenization and where once clothing defined social status and the role in life, now the rich continued to patronize the great design houses, the college students wanted to look like workers and began to adopt the Levis, and clothing no longer labeled the wearer.

Clothing was made for every conceivable use and wardrobes began expanding. There was a very wide range of fashions. Sportwear was a big item at this time, tennis was fashionable, but skating was geared more toward the average person and the costumes are pretty and available. In most of the feminine apparel at this time, in sportswear as well, the waistline was natural and bosoms were accentuated.

The 1930's brought dramatic changes to the fashion picture. The zipper came into wide use and it takes little imagination to realize what its convenience meant, and in 1939 — nylon. The zipper replaced all those buttons or other closures and nylon revolutionized the clothing industry.

Other surprising things came out of the thirties, Hollywood coined some memorable words — 'glamour' was one. It's hard to imagine how we ever lived without the word and harder still to realize it was part of the depression years.

Another faint shock can be felt when reading the women's magazines of 1930. They were devoting many pages to fashion. Perhaps as an antidote to the times. Ski clothes, if you can visualize that, were being touted, "winter sports are becoming more important each year and comfort is the first requisite. Smart women," they said, "are forsaking modernistic designs in favor of somber colors, such as black, navy or brown, the long trouser suits in serge or gabardine or waterproof whipcord with brightly colored accessories, and a heavy woolen shirt should be tucked into the trousers that fit tightly over the hips." It was a somewhat classic look, and while certainly not in tune with the ski clothes of today, could be worn without seeming out of place.

Another publication was promoting "Fashions for the South". These were beach attire which was becoming quite racy, backless, large armholes, no overskirts, with a deep decolletage. Also the one piece tennis dresses, casual lightweight jackets and the long, straight evening wear.

The clothing collector is perfectly justified in seeking out these garments which were worn, for the most part, by people of means, who bought the best and took care of it. The average person wore garments until necessity decreed a replacement and while these are often very easily found, it is a problem to get them in mint condition.

The House of Worth was showing "restaurant" or informal evening wear with low decolletage and low back edged with a band of green and white beads. The materials could be very rich, Worth used brocades and chiffons and velvets. While not everyone can own a Worth, the evening wear of the thirties is what many collectors are seeking. I have recently seen several gowns in excellent condition and prices on clothes of the type have only begun a rather steep rise.

Practical, though, was the word for most day wear. Belts were popular around the normal waistline, skirts flared from the knee down, touches of white at the neck was considered a nice touch. Often you will see these little collars thrown in boxes of unknowing antique shop dealers and you should be alert to what they are.

Wool crepe, which wore well, was used for daytime clothes and velvet predominated at night. The jabot, which was a cascade of frills down the front of the dress or shirt, was high style.

Although collectors have somewhat neglected the 1930's, it was actually a time when fashion had much to commend it. The clothes were fairly simple and practical; bows at the chin, or on one shoulder, or attached low on one hip were a flattering device; the quality was excellent, both as to fabric and finish and they were comfortable. The beret, the cloche, and the 'large, garden-party' hats vied with soft felt, flat staw and the turban.

In our mind's eye, we consider the fashions of the 1930's somewhat dowdy. To those who remember the housedress, a plain, utilitarian garment if ever there was one, but oh, so comfortable and useful, or the everyday dresses of the less affluent, this is understandable, but the better clothing, well made and well designed, hung gracefully on the figure hats or turbans and overlaid with fascinating furs, it could be alluring. It was a style particularly suited to the person with an ingrained sense of elegance and yes, flair. It was essentially a streamlined fashion and much of it is mistaken for clothing of the 20's.

The cloche hats are almost impossible to tell apart, the strap shoes were worn into the thirties, the dresses themselves are often labeled incorrectly and this is where knowledge of waistlines and necklines can be important. This is why, too, anyone who is collecting should try to get any possible information from the dealer and why anyone who is scouring trunks and attics should get the family history.

It is indeed difficult for almost anyone to differentiate clothing made during transitional periods. The styles of the 1928-29 period were already showing the flared skirt, but were shorter, waistlines had risen by 1928-29 but were still lower than those found on the 30's clothes. It becomes increasingly important to the collector to know exactly what the collecting goal is. A lovely, general collection of old clothes, a certain kind of clothing, regardless of period, or, as is always advisable, the clothing of a given time segment. Buy what appeals and is affordable and fit your collection within an overall category of years. Buy what is typical of the period and do not worry overmuch whether the garment or hat was made in 1929 or 1931.

Mail order which really caught on in the 1920's was big business in the 30's and ready-made clothes prospered along with the catalogues. The first fashion illustration ever to appear in such a catalogue was published by Montgomery Ward in 1878. These old catalogues, many in reprint, are wonderful source materials for the collector. When I peruse these, I feel transported back in time and get the urge to pick up the phone and order what I see displayed.

Some of the favorite features of 1930's clothing are still popular, the jabot, the scarf collar which could be tied anyway you pleased, and the lovely deep fur trimmed coats which had the collar set back from the face and yet framed it.

These coats in good condition are bargains at any reasonable price. Well made and beautifully furred and usually wool, they oftentimes cost less than a gown or suit and are lovely to look at, or wear.

If there was one typical daytime style of the 30's it was the print dress. As yet, there are not too many of these available but they should be searched out. Women really loved these bright, cheerful prints, either in small closely spaced figures or medium sized, widely spaced. They often had cape effects or jackets, and for hot weather they were adapted to lighter materials and made sleeveless. This passion for print was one of the characteristics of this time.

Shoes were pumps with bows, or the plain walking pump, or the leather oxford, or the one strap. Kid was the most chosen material, but calf and patent leather were also in favor. Pumps were the favorites, but the reptile skinned shoes made an impact which carried over to later years. The toe could be elongated or pointed and a very attractive type for collectors were the evening shoes with buckle trim, the buckle was part of the shoe itself.

The notable shoe from the 30's was worn for sports activities. It was an oxford with the fringed, outside tongue. This covered the laces and is another of those immediately recognizable styles that can be dated at a glance. Interestingly enough, men's clothing is so scarce that in searching for a collection of men's clothing on any large scale, particularly a comprehensive shoe collection, I sought but did not find.

It was in the 30's that the idea of promoting sales of men's clothing could be based on snob appeal was advanced. Clothing designers and manufacturers have always known that if enough changes are made in garments to render them out of fashion in a short time, more sales will be made as women would rush out to refurbish but this concept had not been widely applied to men's clothes. It was also the time that men began to discard undershirts, supposedly because movie star Clark Gable took off his shirt and only bare chest was visible. Warm shirts in large plaids, and early in the decade the single breasted jacket was the male look. Later, jackets became double breasted and the front of the jacket was higher.

One of the radical changes in women's wear in America during the 30's was the latex girdle. It was flexible and moved with the body and became enormously popular. It was a far cry from the whalebone corset. It was lightweight and could be easily laundered. Even in those days there were obviously some fashion rebels for recently I happened upons several of these girdles unworn, but unfortunately not boxed. "Never were boxed," said the owner, they were bought off store counters and I never wore a girdle at all." These are interesting and if in pristine condition when found, should not yet cost much.

Another drastic change was the neckline. The halter neckline was introduced and caught on. This neckline has survived and prospered, and as with many earlier styles is now being revived by designers and shown on new clothing.

In the late 30's and early 40's traditional modesty was challenged with the introduction of the bare midriff. As with all clever clothing, it was simply an indication of things to come. Fashion always seems to anticipate events.

As net and lacy trifles began to replace hats, the industry quaked. The automobile contributed to the trend, a closed car required no head cover. The hat began to fade as a prime requisite of dress and the industry was further crushed when the Catholic Church announced that feminine head no longer needed to be covered in church. The hat has all but disappeared except for utiliitarian purposes, making the hats of the thirties fine collectibles. Almost the last hurrah of a fashion survivor.

The jewelry of the thirties should be considered just that and has already found a huge market. However, there are certain pieces, such as the dress clips, the belt buckles and the shoe clips of the late 30's which should be added to a clothing collection. The pairs of clips which attached to a dress neckline are particularly desirable. Often this type jewelry is chunky art deco rather than the rare platinum and diamond pieces from the same era. The everyday decorations that women wore have an appeal that is not easily defined, but appeal it does.

Schiaparelli was a product of the thirties and her chief contribution was color – shocking pink became a rage. She had a sense of fun and many of the things she designed seemed outrageous, but she influenced fashion and a Schiaparelli label is something to boast of in a collection. There is a whole new collecting area, not the clothing collector, but the collector of labels in the clothing.

It makes for a surprisingly beautiful collection, the labels are varying sizes and while the new ones are mostly machine woven the older ones are so lovely that the backs resemble needlepoint. The woven ones are much harder to find than they were a year or two ago, the owner of a large collection tells me and "most of them on cheaper clothing are stamped now." If this kind of collection catches on, and already I know of several fine collections, what will happen to the designer-identified gown?

Long beads were still worn at the end of the decade, but chokers lived happily with the V-neckline. The beret was a fitting companion to the slim fitting jackets of the suits, but it was but one of many of the diverse hat styles. America itself was diverse and diversifying, but soon had its course decided for it.

The 1930's were years of depression, then of hope, and finally of war. A stirring ten years, but regardless of other happenings the thirties proves that the influence of fashion goes on.

A real flapper of the 1920's in silk lounging pajamas then all the rage. Typical satin trim. Value $150-200.

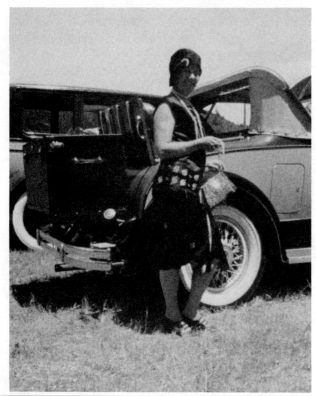

1925 Black satin flapper dress with pink roses embroidered on the lowered waistline. Value $400-500, black felt cloche hat with rhinestone pin. Value $65-95. All contemporary flapper types are busily seeking the cloche. Automobile is a jazzy Reo Flying Cloud.

Knitwear was popular during the early 1920's. This dress is especially interesting because of its bead trim. The top (or blouse) has 100 or more beads which were strung on a ball of yarn and knit into place. The skirt was knitted first and then filled with a tiny wooden mold or other button which would fit. An unusual piece of knitwear. Value $400-500.

The well-dressed tennis player of 1921. Long sweater over blouse and skirt. Since this clothing is difficult to pinpoint as to original use the collector should be guided by existing photographs and documented family history. Value of sweater and skirt which are pictured in shades of old rose $125-150.

Tricotine suit, braid trim, chinchilla standing collar. Value $600-800. Lustrous charmeuse in tunic effect. Attached sash acts as belt, V neck with wide flat collar in back. Scalloped edges. Value $300-400.

1924. All dresses of this year fall into the $275-350 range, unless beaded or unusually designed and decorated.

A richly beaded embroidered silk satin and silk georgette dress. Navy blue and right up to the minute in 1921. These materials as well as the era make dresses of this type much sought after. Value $800-1000.

127

Left to right:

The straight lines of 1921. A one piece slip-on with an adjustable collar, draped at the underarm and has a tie back sash stitched onto the seams. Silk value $200-250.

This has a separate waist with long sleeves, camisole closing at left side front and is joined to a one-piece straight gathered skirt with side tunics. Value $175-200.

Intended for the younger woman, this dress has a separate draped waist closing at the shoulder. The 'Bramley' collar gives it a youthful look. This is jersey cloth with linen collar and cuffs. Value $200-250.

This dress has a kimono-sleeve waist and a 2-piece gathered skirt. Velvet with deep collar of lace. Value $250-400.

Serge. This dress has an embroidered motif on the skirt with collar facings in the same tones, and is a young miss' dress. Value $175-200.

One piece dress with front inset. Scalloped edges of the panel which also boasts braiding. Value of dress in silk is $175-200. Notice the differences in the shoe styles, all being worn in 1921.

If found in good condition, these dresses are all wearable today.

Typical fashions of 1921. Dress for afternoon entertaining, suit with long tunic jacket, wool coat with beaver trim. Dress value $185-225; suit $400-450; coat $800-1,000. Notice shoes.

Left to right: A selection of dresses typical of 1924. All are of linen suiting. Bands of embroidery trim the oval neck, sleeve and front of bodice and skirt. An exotic flower on left side gives the simple dress distinction. Value $350-400.

Lavender with French knot stitching, square neckline and kimono sleeves. Value $350-400.

Rose, green and black embroidery on green runs from neck to hem on left side of dress. Value $350-400.

Greek key border on pongee material gives this dress a coat effect. Value $350-400.

Left: In 1922 Paris decreed a new silhouette. All garments had to be draped, coats, dresses and the new coat dress. Skirts were longer and in most cases fell straight from neck to hem. This coat is softly draped at the low waist with an ornament. Another innovation of that year is shown in this coat with its interlaced stuffed tubing rather than fur to collar and cuff these exclusive garments. Velvet. Value $1,000-1,200.
Center: This dress is of silk and georgette, draped and with lace at the neck and hem. Value $800-1000.
Right: Braided fabric girdles were considered 'interesting' in 1922 and so were the handmade motifs. The braid is evident in the belt and the soft draping makes this dress of softest wool very feminine. Value $800-1000.

Linen suiting, the trim gives this dress a bolero jacket effect. Pockets and side pleats. Value $350-400.

Linen suiting, French knots in blue form the flowers with yellow centers, square neckline side belting, kimono sleeves. Rose linen. Value $350-400.

The Nancy Lopez of 1923 wears a sleeveless sport coat and skirt of cream homespun bordered with rows of yellow, orange and brown lustre wool. Model wears a deep crown wide brim straw hat and comfortable shoes. Value of coat and skirt $195-225.

A 1923 afternoon dress of black and blue chiffon adhering to the straight silhouette. The skirt is pleated at the side with a straight front panel. The intricate sash adds interest to the dress. A very good example of the accessories of the early 1920's. Value of dress $700-800.

A 1923 semi formal frock of faille with georgette. Pleated skirt and overblouse effect. Beautifully simple. Value $700-800.

1927 tea frock. V-neck and cape sleeves. Skirt falls far below the knee. Made from contemporary pattern. Value of original $125-165. Courtesy of Folkwear, San Rafael, California.

Top: A slip on dress of 1924 in **Chinese** design trim. Silk. Wide belt with buckle. Value $500-525. **Cloche hat**, long gloves, fur piece. Bottom: Afternoon dress of silk and chiffon. The cape-like collar extends down the back. Draped on side with bow. Value $500-600. Cloche hat, long gloves, ever-popular pearls.

Flat crepe jumper dress is tailored for street wear and was considered 'serviceable,' a big plus in those years. Value $125-145.

Day dresses of 1926. Printed silk, button trim delineates lowered waistline on left, right dress is belted. Left $135-175. Right $135-175.

Left to right: The clean, lean look of the year 1930. The dresses were essentially flattering to the figure. This has the rippling collar then coming into fashion. The pleating builds up the top of the silhouette and makes the hips slimmer by comparison. The gores in the skirt stress the slenderness and height. Sheer sleeves. Value of 30's clothing is increasing rapidly as collectors realize its clever tailoring and easy wearing qualities. Dress $200-250. The coat of this sheer frock and coat ensemble hangs in loose, easy lines because the dress has a cape collar trimmed with pleating and because the skirt has gores which contrive the new slight flare. Value $300-350. The Paris influence of 1930 is evident in this wool belted tunic. Under the coat the dress has enormous gathered sleeves. Slender shawl collar and again the restrained flare. Value $350-400. This ensemble with its contrasting colors and materials was known as "print and plain". The chic so evident in much 30's clothing is very apparent here. The confetti printed silk is used generously to liven the free-swinging wool coat and the wool is repeated in the sash to accent the frock. Value $350-400. The hat styles are typical of the period as are the pumps.

Young lady's prom dress of 1939. Pink taffeta with velvet trim, sweetheart neckline, puff sleeves. Value $125-145.

1930 checked cotton in white, green, blue, with bot- m of skirt cut on the bias and capelet sleeves, often distinguishing feature of 30's clothing. Buttons in nt, belted. Value $150-200; white crocheted gloves, vy blue straw cloche. The great cloche hunt is on, s probably the most desired hat style which collec- s are seeking.

1930's chiffon print dinner dress, purple, cerise print. Black lace bodice over a taffeta slip, removable bolero jacket which ends in lace and becomes the belt. Snap closure at the side, bias-cut skirt, it does not have a train but is made long to hang evenly on the floor. Value $350-450.

135

The remarkable low back dress of September, 1930 is a genuine classic. This is satin. Value $500-600.

These are 'Hoover dresses' of 1931. Linen and gingham, sleeveless, easy to slip on tying behind with long belt in a bow knot. They could also be worn over more formal wear if necessary to dash into the kitchen. They were usually one size, considered a 'house dress' or overall apron. These inexpensive items reflect the same styling as some more expensive dresses, the slight flare, the attention to detailing, and the flattering neckline. Value $45-75.

Pure silk pongee dress with dainty pipings on the cuffs, vestee and hipline. Crepe collar, full circular skirt, self material belt. One of the great attributes of silk pongee was its ability to launder well. The neat look of the thirties is evident here. Value $145-185.

Dresses of the 1930's were made in very fine materials. The dress on the left is of pure linen with a peplum at the waist, the cuffs of the short sleeves are piped in contrasting color. The skirt has large box pleats and 2 inverted pleats in the front. Loose belt with a composition buckle. The dress on the right was a very popular model. Patterned crepe with georgette collars and cuffs edged with lace. The skirt has box pleats both front and back and is piped with colors to match. The jumper skirt is made of all wool French spun non-sag jersey with a novelty box pleat in front. Loose belt with a metal buckle. Dresses of this quality and style are in the $150-200 range.

One of the charms of the clothing of the 1920's is its sculptured quality and purity of line which is very apparent in these dresses. The whole look was simple yet sexy. The lowered waistline, the side draping with large bows, the pleating, all lend an air of decoration without interfering with the basic line. Dresses of this type of the 1920 period are moving into the $650-850 price range depending on materials and trim. They are eminently wearable and are eagerly sought after. As beaded dresses of the period are disappearing into collections the more available fancy day dresses and less spectacular evening wear is moving up in price. 1928.

Left to right: 'Prints' were the rage in the 1930's. Left is 'print cloth' with organdy trim. Black bow tie, shirred waistline. Self belt ties in back. Value $95-125. Printed pongee with criss-cross collar, flare cuffs, belt has metal buckle, circular skirt with inverted pleats. Value $95-125. Printed broadcloth with Russian tunic effect, a wildly popular style, cuffs, collar, piping of white broadcloth. Grosgrain tie, trimmed with pearl buttons. Skirt pleated front and back, value $100-145. Two piece dress of linen. Silk streamer tie. Skirt has contrasting color piping around the hips and two inverted pleats. Pearl buttons. Value $135-155. Crepe dress has short puff sleeves for a youthful look. Embroidered and hemstitched organdy collar and plain rayon bow tie. Flared skirt with flounce at bottom. Value $95-125. These dresses run the gamut of materials and trims and are indicative of the often unusual combinations during these years.

A stunning creation of rayon canton crepe. This is the 'long' length and has lace in the sleeves which are puffed by elastics and shirred at the top. Neckline is softened by tucks in front melting into folds and heightened by a self flower. Skirt is seamed and flared in back with waist seamings at the front only. Incredible tailoring considering the price of the garments originally. Value $450-500.

All silk crepe-back satin, fine lace over an eggshell lining forming a rather ingenious drop-shouldered, star pointed yoke. Shirred sleeves held puffed by the lining. Covered buttons, rhinestone pins, belt has slide. Provocative. Value $600-750.

The capelet was another distinguishing feature of the 30's clothes. This dress is of silk crepe satin, which shimmered in the light. White undercapelets and flower trim set off the sleek simplicity of the gown. Another dramatic dress dress essentially langourous in feeling. Value $600-750.

140

All wool 'swagger suit' tweed, with an unlined jacket. Cartridge-tucked sleeves, drop shoulders, the usual Ascot throw with pin. Value $300-350.

Although these dresses of the 1933-34 period are made in a fitted style they are often found in large sizes, as is the case with this 2 piece ensemble of wool crepe. Shoulders were emphasized in this two tone dress with jacket with stitched epaulets. Attached 'throws' tie in ascot fashion. Dress is belted with the usual prominent buckle and has button trim. Value $300-350.

Clockwise from upper left: All rayon canton crepe in medium blue with lighter blue top. The material looks much like silk. Button trimmed collar, belt with typical 30's buckle. Value $100-125. Celanese taffeta party dress with detachable sleeves. Coral rose with self-colored embroidery on the scalloped collar. The sleeves were kept in place with elastics. This type dress can be remembered by anyone who lived through the 30's. Value $150-175. Center: Navy blue dress with military epaulets and shiny metal buttons is made of printed cotton 'tweedy' suiting material. Value $85-125.
Silk flat crepe in red with harmonious prints and eggshell trim. Self belt with bow. Value $85-125. Velveteen 'best' dress for a young child. Sleeves and picoted bud-trimmed collar of silk flat crepe. Contrasting hand smocking at front. Value $95-135. Brown wool and cotton flannel suit called a 'swagger suit' which in this case applies more to the swing of the skirt than the jacket. Jacket unlined, skirt plain at back and each can be worn with other garments. Value $100-145. Collectors of older garments all or partially made of wool need to check condition very carefully.

Top right two dresses: $95-155 value range.

Above two dresses: $95-145 value range.

These three right dresses: 1935. Cape effects were widely used in 1935-1936 and 1937. Dresses of this type as shown in this 1935 advertisement were designed for the woman who was "36 or more", on up to size 50. Dresses of this type range $95-155 if short, long gowns range $175-200. Dresses of this era are beginning to be avidly sought after.

142

Left to right: 1935. Cotton suits were chic for summer. Jackets of this type were generally about 25" long, the skirt about 32" long. White with black and white check was popular, as in this houndstooth example. Jacket unlined, skirt is plain in back. Value $95-125.

This suit is of woven nubbed cotton suiting, with slim line, unlined jacket featuring the ultra modish, almost mannish peak lapels. Patch pockets and fancy buttons. Value $95-125.

This is a coat and skirt ensemble. The coat is about 40" long. White and black check of cotton honeycomb suiting. The neck interest is evident in these fashions. Suits of this kind are still undervalued. Value $150-195.

Dresses were nicely detailed in 1939 and furs often carried for effect rather than warmth. 'Tubize' was a new fabric made of rayon yarn. If any clothing you own bears a label with this designation it can be dated exactly. Beautiful pleating and tucks are featured in these dresses. Both are belted and one is buttoned down the front. Both models sport fur hats, one carries a muff, the other a shoulder fur. Dresses such as these are valued at $95-125 and are finally coming into their own. Most flattering styles, and tailoring is superior in dresses of this era. Fur muff, mink, value $250-275, fur piece, mink, $175-200.

1920's evening coat, black, reversible satin and crepe with flaring cape sleeves. This 20's coat is shorter than the 30's dress the model is wearing. Value of coat $250-325.

1921, winter styles. All wool coat with wide belt, chinchilla trim and muff. Dashing military look. Value $1,000-1,200.

Early 1920's grey-blue silk velvet coat with chinchilla trim. Silk crepe lining. Weighted in hem. Value $2000-2700.

Fur trimmed coats were de rigueur in 1933-34. Often the fur was wolf-blended dog fur as in this case. Coat is dark brown with black fur. Value $300-350.

This coat is made of suede coating material which is about 2/3 wool and has an interesting diagonal weave and is trimmed with a profusion of rich looking fur-effect fabric resembling lapin fur. Lined and interlined. Belted. Value $250-300.

Short evening coat of 1938. Rose colored taffeta, rayon lining. Original rhinestone pin. Originally worn to a school dance in 1938, worn again recently with equal panache. Value $95-125.

Monkey coat, 1939-1940. Silk lining, corde collar. Value $1750-2000.

Ocelot jacket, 1939. $650-750.

Striped beaver coat of the 1930's. $900-1200.

146

Woman's raccoon coat, full length. In excellent condition the value is $995-1200.

1938. Hooded raincoat, processed cotton gabardine, double breasted, worn with high boots and fur lined kid gloves. Since these are still wearable, timeless and often found in excellent condition they are somewhat difficult to date. Value $45-55.

A particularly graceful chiffon beaded dress with large bow. 1923. Value $650-850.

*Point Ada "*

*atron.*

*ilton*

A spectacular formal costume intended for an installation ceremony in 1924. Lace dress with side panels, scalloped hemline, narrow shoulder straps. Value $750-1,000. The headdress certainly commands attention. Value $125-150. Satin shoes, large bouquet.

The 1923 silhouette. An afternoon gown of black crepe Roma with sleeves set in from the waistline. The unusual drapery drops from the shoulder at the back on the right side, but from the waistline only on the left. Panels of embroidery. Dress $800-850. Wonderful hat.

Little soutache 'pancakes' of graduated sizes are the only decoration on this afternoon dress. The draped girdle is self material. Black crepe Roma. Value $800-850.

The design of this dress is most interesting. It is 'built' of wide brown satin ribbon combined with narrow bands of embroidery worked with antique gold thread in outline and single stitch. Fluted ribbons form the collar and cuffs and a big soft bow is used at the left front of the dress. Value $800-850.

Black silk sateen 'dressy' dress, very early 1920's. Front and side gathers form drapes which not only catch the eye but form the dress to a flattering fit. Knee length. The long V shaped dickey snaps into place on the dress itself and when removed and the dress worn without it, the garment takes on an entirely different look. This dress, which does not have a label, exemplifies the fact that good tailoring recurs in every fashion cycle – it is made in much the same way as earlier clothing and this attention to detail is also found in surprising numbers of later dresses and coats. Value $450-650.

Evening dress of brown chiffon with fine lace and ribbon inserts. The skirt is cut on the bias, belted with a rhinestone buckle. This is a particularly interesting garment – the color, the way the lace is inserted and the sleeves are all of unusual interest. c. 1930. Value $750-850.

Large size bugle beaded dress of the 1920's. Black, silver and gold beads on black. Lined with black satin. A stunning dress, eminently wearable. $1,000-1,500.

Black satin and pink chiffon 1920's beaded dress. Beading on front attached panel only. Value $500-600.

1920's satin beaded dress. Two piece, large size, skirt lined. extremely heavy. Value $650-850.

1920's Beaded Dress. Sequin and beaded short dress, black and blue sequins form large swirls, tiny black beads fill in as well as forming the bodice which is chiffon. Net bottom and all lined. Side opens with snap, front and back panel lift so skirt can be raised to ensure no damage from sitting. Value $550-750.

Left to right: Silk crepe, c. 1930, chocolate brown long sleeve beaded dress worn with a fur neckpiece. Value of dress $250-300.

Royal blue chiffon cocktail dreess, c. 1929-31, the V-neck sleeveless gown with back and front rhinestone design, the lower skirt with multiple panels and uneven hemline. A striking dress. Value $600-750. The model is carrying a blue and gold evening coat with white fox collar, some renovation, labeled the HALLE BROTHERS COMPANY, CLEVELAND, OHIO. Value $150-250.

Iridescent green lace cocktail dress with brown underslip and chiffon sleeves, c. 1920-1930. Value $300-350.

Cocktail dress, c. 1930, black net lace with velvet trim. Worn with black velvet pearl-trimmed tiara, and a bead-bordered silk tulle stole. Value of dress $400-450.

This costume has an ecru silk skirt lined with lightweight wool. A ribbon draws the skirt to a bustle in the back. The waist is ecru crocheted with a high neck with pearl button trim. Draw string reticule and brown velvet hat with plume. Value of dress $500-650. The gentleman's very formal tails with black tie is contemporary. All mens' formal wear is highly collectible.

152

Lounging garments continued to be popular. In 1931 the kimono was high style. This was generally called a 'lounging robe' and is ornamented with little tufts of cotton. Slender tie belt. Value of robe $75-95. The pajama costume is decorated on only one leg and on the opposite side of the blouse front. The blouse could be worn inside or out. These lounging pajamas are rather difficult to find but well worth the effort. Value in silk $150-175.

Pongee pajamas, favorites in the early '20s. Value $125-150.

Left: French embroidered lingerie of 1923. A sleeveless nightgown of sheer, soft white batiste in the empire style with inset yoke sections at back and front. Embroidered with a dainty rose spray. Value $200-250.

Right: A brassiere and skirt combination of heavy white sateen. The brassiere is embroidered in white, shoulder straps of cotton tape. Skirt is gored, lightly gathered and joined to the brassiere. Value $150-200.

1931 rayon crepe pajamas, 'trousers' have pleated insets, V yoke front and elastic at back. Blouse has self bindings around neck and armholes. Embroidery. Value $150-175. Dress of good quality voile for little girl. Capelet sleeves, pleated down the front, embroidered with roses. 1931. Value $45-65.

Top, left to right: Lingerie was pretty and rather alluring in 1933. Girls up to 14 wore cotton broadcloth bloomers with nainsook slip, although even in lesser fabrics the construction was the same as in the more expensive silks. Value of bloomers $10-12; value of slip in girls' size $15-20. These are usually called lounging pajamas but were in fact worn around the house for general use, to do housework, to 'romp' in, or 'to exchange secrets with your girl friend.' The butterfly sleeves were new in 1933 and the cotton broadcloth print attractive. One piece style. Value $95-150. The slip is crepe cut in fitted style, lace trim. Flesh color, value $35-40. All silk crepe chemise. Fitted style, trimmed with rosebuds and lace. Flesh pink or peach were the usual colors. Value $35-50.

Pajamas of soft finish longcloth, hand embroidered. Pink, peach or Nile green, Empire waist. Value $100-150. The gown hangs loose and has a sash, also hand embroidered. Value $75-85.

155

Child's French satin bed garment. Lace and satin, rosette at neckline. Made in Paris. Value $100-145.

Lounging pajamas, 1920's, 50 percent silk, 50 percent rayon, machine made lace sewn onto pajamas. Value $125-150.

1930's 'Satin Dache' panties, buttoned on side. Darker lace trim. Unworn. $30-40.

Rayon jersey petticoat chemise. Fits snug to be worn under sheer frocks but is full below the hips. Value $35-50.

Underthings of 1924: Camisole tops: silk, $95-110; cotton, $55-65. Corsets of this period: $40-45. Combinations (bottom row) $45-50. These are characteristics of the 20's silhouette.

Below: An embroidered batiste camisole of 1923. Value $45-55.
Step-in panties which match the camisole. Value $35-50.

An array of cordsets, 1939. Top left - 'high' corset with matching bra. The 'high' effect controls a 'roll'. Center top - corselette for half sizes; top right - this girdle controls the 'young' figure; bottom left - short front lacing decreases waistline; bottom center - softly boned elastic top nips waistline; bottom right - girdle with matching bra pulls in waist. All of these were used to nip in here and push in there but often they are found in their original boxes or bags indicating women were not so anxious to submit to these tortures. An untapped collecting field. Value $25-50.

Full length kimono, 1920's. Black damask silk, raised embroidered flower design of mums, daisies and rosebuds on the back and partially on the front, in colors of red, yellow-green and white. The gold silk lining has a circular design enclosing a flower at the back neckline. The owner says it was originally worn by her grandmother who was "tall and stately". These kimonos are elegant and comfortable. Values are rising quickly. $350-375.

Back detail of kimono showing gorgeous embroidery.

Short kimono, very fine silk, black background with colorful floral and bird design 'mums' in orange, blue, green, tan, red and gold; daisies in pink and brown shades. Placking trim is flowered design. Both back and front have beautiful spray arrangements of flowers. Orange silk lining. Detachable sleeves. Probably from Franklin Simon's New York. 1920's. Value $350-375. 122

Light blue rayon jacquard trimmed with lace. Child's christening coat, worn around 1925. Value $110-125.

160

Black crepe underdress, sleeveless tunic of gold silk brocade, 1930's. Value $250-300. This dress has been worn recently with great success. Necklace of faux pearls and green glass beads is also 30's vintage.

Printed cotton smock, once a popular utility garment. This was worn in 1935. Three-quarter length, buttons down front, ties at the wrist. Value of these rather uncommon articles of clothing often stem from the interesting old printed fabrics from which they were made. Value $25-35.

Blouses have wide price variations. This type, $45-65.

Summer of 1921. Slip-on blouses were in style and were often worn with white cotton skirts. Embroidery was a prominent trim. This blouse is of jade green cotton crepe, embroidered in henna. The lines are outlined in henna, the belt is a 'string girdle'. Value $150-175.

1921. A slip-on overblouse with long set-in sleeves, the fullness at the waist is confined with a ribbon drawn through button-holed eyelets under the embroidery. Scalloped edged. White voile. Beautiful addition to a collection. Value $300-350. The parasol is of white poplin with embroidery to match the blouse. Value $200-225. Matching hat $185-195.

Two hats of 1921, they are large and lacy. Left, cutwork over heavy linen with wide ribbon band and bow; right, white embroidered net over pink linen. These hats are not always dated correctly, but they were enormously popular in the early 20's. Value $195-225.

Clockwise starting top left: Hats of Spring, 1925. The large, flattering brim. A charming combination of hand embroidered silk with fine straw. **Value $200-250.** Fruit and flower appliques in vivid colors on straw. **Value $150-200.** Tailored straw hat of pedal straw trimmed with satin, and a jade motif. **Value $175-200.** Three tiers of little scarlet flowers on a velvet trimmed hat of cherry straw. **Value $150-185.** This hat has an interesting under-brim trimming of brilliant applique motifs subdued by a veilling of tulle. **Value $125-250.** The flapper hairdos, pearls, feather boas, the very poses are entirely representative of the period. No wonder every female is yearning for a collection of 20's clothing.

Counterclockwise, starting top left: Easter hats of 1925. Mata Hari could have worn this deep crowned straw trimmed with ribbon and lace. No one would have ever recognized her. Still it's a fantastic hat. Value $200-250. What was "ultra new" in 1925, a cluster of roses placed as to widen the brim of this straw hat. Value $200-250. 1925 version of the graceful Directoire poke with much maligned visor front. Women complained that this made it difficult to see around them. Value $225-250. A compact brim covering of flowers, widening into picturesque wing sections at the sides. Ribbon trim on top of crown. Value $225-250. Another poke, trimmed with flowers and crepe. Value $225-250. In 1925 the afternoon hat was a necessary accessory. This stunning creation has a hair crown and crepe brim in pastel tints, trimmed with a cluster of American beauty roses. Value $250-300.

An array of the most sought after type of hat of the 1920's, the toque. Counterclockwise: These are all of felt, although they can be found in straw, silk and other materials. Hat at top is a bolero toque with irregular brim revers laced with narrow ribbon; a life-sized poinsettia and torsades of felt add interest to the Pierrot shape with upturned brim; Two piece crown with slashed and folded brim; felt torsades and felt petals, petals in contrasting shade of green; collapsible toque with tailored trimming of felt; felt strips take the place of soutache and form a scroll design on a tall-crowned polo toque. Value of hats of this kind and of this period is rising and should begin at $125 and increase according to material, trim and general attractiveness.

Left: Hats of the 1933-35 period are wonderful additions to a collection and are quite neglected. Prices are 'right' and they are fairly easy to find. Rayon-faced velvet with a feather ornament and veil. This veil, like many of that time, is embroidered. Value $30-35. This adjusts to individual head size. Knitted cotton 'headhugging' turban and ascot scarf set. Rings decorate turban. These sets were popular and not often found together today. Value as a set $45-55. The turban is an enduring fashion note.

Right, top to bottom: Deep ridged crown of wool felt, two tone grosgrain ribbon trim, turned-down brim. Value $35-45. This hat was intended specifically for 'large heads.' Wool felt with ridged or creased crown. Two tone satin ribbons, a feather quill, tail coverts, veil. Value $35-45. Large head size model, this hat is of wool crepe, grosgrain ribbon, lacquered ornament simulates feathers. Value $25-30.

Accessories, 1920's, 1930's. Left to right: hat stand, top covered in velvet with rhinestones, c. 1920, value $30-35. Hat form, painted with bobbed hair, c. 1928, $35-45. Rhinestone necklace, hand set stones. $40-50. Rhinestone bag, chain handles, c. 1930's. $75-80. Garters, 1920's each, $22-27. Satin shoes, ankle straps, buttons, c. 1919, $70-80. Cigarette holder, $40-50.

167

The transitional influence of the late 1920's is shown in the hat worn by this elegant lady of 1930. The 'silver foxes' are still considered one of fashion's classic statements. Silver fox furpiece value $500-750; hat $95-110.

"Silver foxes" worn over 30's velvet dress. Net and velvet bow headpiece, c. 1936-37. Fur piece, $500-750. Net 'hat'. This has no frame so is considered a veil. $20-25.

Accessories of the 1920's. Top - feather headpiece worn low on the forehead, perfect with a beaded dress. 1920's value $55-75; middle row, left - shoe buckles, cut steel, marked "France" $50-75; hand set rhinestone shoe buckles, 1930's $45-50; cut steel in an unusual shape, marked "made in France" value $50-75, lower line filagree metal of the 1930's $15-20; bottom row - art deco shoe clips, green and white $35-50; rhinestone and pearl shoe clips of the 1940's $12-15; bow shoe clips of metallic mesh of the early 1930's $25-35. All shoe buckles are rising in price. Shoe buckles are one of the most stunning collectibles, specialization is the key to a fine collection of these, but collecting can begin on any price level.

168

Fancy apron, 1930's, hand embroidered, $35-50.

1931. Long scarf, $25-27. Shorties scarves and ties, $20-25.

1928. This is an apron of the slip over the head type. It has a back to the waist and is seamed at the shoulders. Bias fold binding, two deep pockets. Aprons are still an untapped mine of interesting, unusual and often beautifully constructed clothing. Cotton, embroidered. Value $20-30.

Below: 'Smartest' shoe worn in the Fall and Winter of 1921. It has 'snap and pep.' Combination patent leather and kid finish. Uppers are soft black dull kid finished leather and are stitched in white. Patent leather tip, ball strap design. Patent leather front lace stay and 'wave' top. Concave military heel. Value $100-145. Shoes in perfect condition continue to be elusive.

1930's hat with rhinestone pin. Velvet and satin $35-45; peach colored nubby cotton, leather-trimmed shoes of the early 30's $50-60; 1920's black satin button strap shoes $45-55; black leather slipper, lined with satin, front bow $30-35, 1930's. In a short period of time I have put together a collection of women's house slippers (almost all unworn) which has proved quite pretty and rewarding and inexpensive. 1930's never worn light brown soft leather button strap shoes with a rather incongrous bow in front. Value $50-60; 1930's very collectible rhinestone slipper value $85-100. Rhinestones all hand set in deep wells to resist scuffing; snake skin handbag of the 1930's, leather lined with a black and gold art deco handle. These reptile handbags are one of the really rising collectibles. Value $125-145; evening bag of black velvet from the 1930's, self-handle on back, rhinestone clasp. Value $65-95.

Silk satin shoes with cut steel buckles, c. 1928-29, known to have been worn in 1929. Often the shoes are being bought by collectors of buckles. Value $75-85.

1930's shoes (unworn), $50-60.

Shoes present difficulties to the collector unless they are unworn or nearly so. These were the types popular in 1934-35. Heels were varied, the so-called spike was not the same as the heel we bring to mind at the use of that term, the 'Cuban' was also called 'continental Cuban' and flats were also popular. The same shoe could also be had in different heel types. Value of shoes of this era in excellent condition $45-75.

The shoe most identified with young girls during the 1930's. Soft, shiny patent with buckle. Rubber cushioned heels. Value $35-40.

Girls shoes, 1933. Black with gray and silver colored trim. Colonial styled slipper with slightly tapered toe and covered heel. Value $25-35.

Shiny patent leather with open cut outs and applique of black reptile effect and silver colored leather. Value $30-35.

Bathing beauty of 1924. Wool bathing suit, one piece, skirted, bathing slippers of rubber, bathing socks. The accessories would be a tremendous find, the suit $65-85.

A couple of bathers in 1924. She wears a one piece wool suit with red and white check material at bodice and end of bloomers. Rubber bathing cap and shoes. Man wears one piece suit, wool, with black bottom and white top. Also wears shoes. Although early ads refers to the footwear as shoes, people who wore them tell me they were generally referred to as 'bathing slippers.' Bathing suits, each $65-85. Bathing slippers $30-50. Since both caps and slippers were of rubber, they are not readily available.

Black sateen bathing suit of 1923. It has an applique of orchid and purple and has purple piping around the sleeves, neck and cap. The cap matches and is of double sateen. A tight fitting rubber cap was worn under this headgear.

The bathing beauties of the 1920's exude sensuality in spite of the modesty of the garment itself. Some of the suits were belted, others were two piece with long tops without belts. They were made of cotton rib knit, 100% pure worsted wool, jersey knit and came in a variety of patterns and colors. Not too many of these seem to have survived and they are eminently collectible. Value of these types of adult suits $65-85. Child's value $35-45.

Elaborate formal wedding of 1928. The satin and lace concept was never more evident, the size of the bouquet, which was typical of those years, is not only eye catching but magnificent. Dozens of satin ribbons hang from the bouquet, the imported lace veil is worn low on the forehead and is trimmed with wax orange blossoms. The lace veil is worn over an underveil of fine net. The dress is chiffon and lace and tiered. Satin shoes. This truly ornate and beautiful costume has become a family heirloom, worn by other brides. Value of the veil is $750-1000, the gown $650-1000. The groom wears the requisite formal morning costume for such a wedding.

Clothing for children of the early 1930's, typical styles made of broadcloth, linen, wool spun jersey, cotton, crepe de chine, and pongee. The little boys' suits range in value from $35-50; the little girls' dresses $45-95; and the dresses for young teenagers (who never realized that was what they were back then) are valued at $100-150.

175

1936. Young girl's party dress. Taffeta with attached belt. Value $125-245.

Girl's batiste lingerie dress of the 1920's. Lace inserts, dropped waist and dropped shoulders. The great attribute of these 'lingerie' dresses was their ability to withstand many launderings. Value $100-145. Large white hair bow. Late 1920's, early 1930's. The dropped waistline can also be found on much earlier clothing.

A graduation frock, Spring 1921. Crisp white organdy. All edges except the bottom of the skirt are bound with bias binding and it has an organdy rose at the waist. Double apron panels are mounted over a plain foundation. The waist is attached to the skirt, has set-in sleeves and an outer panel to match the skirt. Embroidered. This is a very desirable dress. Value $500-600.

Girls' wear, 1924.
Dresses, $50-60.
Coat $75-100.

Spring of 1931 fashions for children. All of these are made of cotton so they could be laundered easily. Much of the decoration is the 'tucking' but in the 'ensemble' the skirt and blouse are joined together underneath the hip band. It is sleeveless and worn with the cloche hat. The dresses are short as is the hairstyle. Values of children's dresses of the early 1930's depends on the correct time attribution, often this is difficult. Some of these dresses were worn with matching bloomers and when the hipline is defined the dating becomes easier. Good quality with careful tailoring and good trim dresses are valued at $100-125.

177

A variety of clothing made for children. Clockwise: Child's rompers with waist. Suspenders attached. Waist closes at back. Trim on waist matches pants. Cotton value $45-65

Bloomer dress. Embroidered puppy on band. Gingham with white banding. Value $65-75.

This girl's dress has kimono sleeves, a one piece gathered skirt and closing at left side of vest. Girls up to 14 years of age wore these. Value in voile. $150-185.

The wonderful middy dress which has never really gone out of style. The one piece pleated skirt is joined to an underwaist which closes at the back. Value with original tie $150-175.

Empire slip made for girls up to 12 years. Two piece skirt is joined to the Empire waist and slips over the head. Nainsook. Value $45-65. Notice polka dot socks.

Pleated bloomer for the miss up to 16 years old. Value $75-95.

Combination undergarment for young girls. Bloomer style. Cotton. Value $100-120.

One piece slip on frock closing at the back with skirt gathered to long waist. Skirt panels are turned under. Value $95-125.

178

This girl's dress is made of blue suiting with white repp vest, collar and cuffs. Worn by girls 4 to 8 years of age. 1921. Value $145-165.

'Cherry Ripe' outfit for a little girl. White swiss with bright red dots, bound with scarlet bias binding which outlines the petal skirt panels and kimono sleeves. 'Dutchy' collar. Round hat with deep crown matches the dress. Red cherries dangling from waist give the costume its name. Value of set $165-185.

All wool beret and slip-over V-neck sweater. Hand embroidered boat and signal and flag design. All wool coat sweater, fancy striping and hand embroidered boat and birds. Sweaters of this vintage in good condition should be valued at $30-35.

Another romper suit of the early 1920's. Yellow Japanese crepe with a hand embroidered duck on front. It buttons down the back. The guimpe is of thin white cotton. These were worn by boys up to 6 years of age. $45-65.

1920 rompers. This is an 'Oliver Twist' romper suit of linen. Value $100-125. To find the scooter would be a bonus.

Boy's suit and cap, 1920. Tan soisette blouse, pique cuffs, collar and trousers. Cap is pique. Suit $95-125, cap $35-40.

The boys wear of 1922 seems remarkably dated. Boy at left wears a crochet slip on sweater, worn with knickerbockers, bow tie and collar. The cap is shetland wool knit. Sweater $20-25. A coat sweater of wool worn with a peaked cap. Sweater buttons are oversized, boy-sized pockets. Value $20-25.

Boy's all wool single breasted suit, winter weight. The coat has a twill lining, knickerbockers are also lined. Brown. The cap matches the suit. Suit value is $100-125.

Girl's middy style dress, all wool serge. Pleated, trimmed with white braid and has silk embroidered emblem on the sleeve. Navy blue. Value of these which are scarce $150-175. Matching tam-o-shanter, value $30-40.

Dress 34B60

Boy's suit of 1930. Wool, knickerbockers, wool socks, oxfords, the cap was the popular headgear. Suit value $75-95.

1933. Everyday dress for children in the early 1930's. The boy wears woolen knickerbockers, short wool jacket and aviator cap. The girl's coat is wool with a small fur collar, beret and she carries a school bag with strap over the shoulder. Clothing of this ordinary kind is rather difficult to find and not yet widely collected. Values are dependent on condition, quality and desirability.

1926-1932. Men's knickers, wool, buckled at side of band below the knee. Golfers gave knickers a sporty image. Value $45-55.

Little boys in 1931. Suits of short pants with attached waists. The pants, even in this length, were generally referred to as 'trousers'. These are of flannel with a cotton waist. Suit $35-40. The romper suit was worn by boys up to 6 years of age. This is gingham and it is difficult to visualize a large 6 year old boy wearing such a costume. Value $35-45.

A variety of clothing made for children. From left: Children's wear 1924. Value of dress $50-55. Value of suspenders, $55-75. Little girl's coat with matching deep crowned hat. Value $95-110. Bloomer dress, gingham with white banding. Value $55-75. Value suit $55-75. Right boy wears cotton shirt with cotton belted short trousers. Value $45-55.

Kiddie clothes of 1933. For the 3 to 6 year old girl, dotted organdy party dress, value $25-30. Printed cotton broadcloth with a matching pocketbook dog. Value $30-35. Flowered summer organdy with matching hat and purse, value as a set $55-60. Dotted Swiss with matching hat, value of set $35-45. Voile dress with the attractive crinkle fabric called Plisse crepe at the collar and cuffs, value $30-40. Party dress rosette trimmed ruffled dress of all rayon taffeta, value $65-75.

During certain past eras children were dressed exactly as their elders, but during the 30's the clothing of youngsters was attractive, comfortable and appropriate. Little boys wore tailored suits of broadcloth such as the one on the left which has plain colored pants with a candy striped waist with white trim. Value $25-35; romper suit also made of broadcloth with picot edged organdy trim with embroidery and elastic at the legs. This suit opens at the bottom, Value $35-45; pique romper made in a double breasted style, collar and cuffs trimmed with organdy, opens at the bottom, pearl buttons. Value $35-45; little girl's dress of silk pongee. This is a party dress with a hand embroidered collar and hand smocked yoke, tiny capelet sleeves and a deep hem. Value $45-65; fine checked gingham print with organdy trim. Fastens down the front with colored buttons. The apron is white organdy with matching gingham print trim fastens under the collar and ties in the back. Set $45-60.

Underwear from the thirties worn by little tykes is rarely found in good condition. This is a Ruben's vest, knit and was warm and comfortable. It is 50% wool, 50% silk. Value $10-15. The same Ruben's vest made of high grade rayon striped cotton and wool. Value $5-7.50; slip-over type, rayon shell edges $2-5.

Baby caps and bonnets: Left to right: rayon taffeta bonnet, frilled and shirred. Embroidered organdy bonnet trimmed with silk ribbon and embroidery. Rosette trimmed bonnet of rayon taffeta. Silk crepe de chine bonnet, shirred and puffed, turned up front. Bonnets have a value of $35-65 each.

Infants' outfits of the 1920's. The bonnet is batiste, all one piece with the front turning back to form a rever. Tuck outlines the crown which forms a casing for the ribbon. Pin tucks decorate the crown. Batiste is often used for these and can be quite sheer. Embroidered. Value $45-65.

Below: An all-wool flannel petticoat. One seam, scalloped and embroidered. The neckline is trimmed with tatting. Value $65-85.

Above: The little dress is fine silk finish batiste. The bottom of the skirt is trimmed with lace. The neck and sleeves are finished in lace. Beautiful workmanship on all these garments puts them in the heirloom category. Value of dress. $175-200.

This coat is heavy white silk crepe de chine with hand embroidered collar and cuffs in the rambler rose pattern. The fullness at the top of the skirt portion comes from two box pleats. It has French knots of silk and bow knots of ribbon. The ribbon which fastens the neck has a jade bead. Value $200-250.

183

Childrens' shoes in 1933. Blucher oxford, white linen with open mesh vamp; strap pumps in patent leather; leather sandles; black elk leather for both boys and girls; patent leather swing strap; sturdy oxfords; dressy patent leather strap model. Children's shoes of this era are not yet widely collected. Value of these types $25-40.

The men's suits in keeping with the times project a macho image. Boys and mens suits valued $65-85.

Trench coat. A 'rain or shine' garment of double textured rubberized cotton gabardine with a plaid lining, two welt slant pockets and a belt finished with a ring fastener. Trench flap, leathere covered buttons. Dashing then, dashing now. Value $150-175.

In 1933 the men were considered fashionable when their trouser bottoms measured 22 inches. The primary colors were dark blue, oxford gray, and medium brown. A 'nifty,' dapper style boasted one button closing, broad 'rope' shoulders and peak lapels. Wool with subdued small check two tone pattern with flecks. Value $150-175. 100% virgin wool suit of herringbone weave with harmonizing chalk-line stripes. Two button closing, tie and handkerchief match and were sold with the suit. Value $150-175.

1927. Knickers worn by college types with plaid knee socks and casual tie shoes. Wool knickerbockers, value $45-55.

1922. A knitted vest with a back and trimmings of tan. This golfer also wears a plaid cap, tie and long trousers. Vest value $65-85.
1922. The lightweight slip-on sweater in camel's hair was worn for sports under a coat. Since knit sweaters are still very much the same today this would be a difficult item to date exactly unless the provenance were known. $35-40. This tennis buff looks quite contemporary.

1930. 'Stetson' has become almost a generic term in men's fashion. This Homberg was made by Stetson and was known as the 'Stetsonian' model. It has a 'jaunty curve suitable for semi-formal occasions'. A dressy hat with a welt-edge brim with three rows of stitching. Hats of this type have become the rage among young men. Value with the Stetson label $45-55.

Snap brim style men's hats of 1933-34. Wool felt, usually with grosgrain band but sometimes these are found with leather bands. These hats are catching on and becoming a desirable, wearable collectible among young men. Value $25-30.

Men's Hats from the 1920's to 1950's, beaver felt. Values $30-50.

Men's shoes were less ornamented than those of younger boys. These are valued at $30-35 pair.

Square toes were what boys wore in 1933. Shoes of this type in good condition are valued at $30-35. They are not yet widely collected and are difficult to find without signs of wear.

# CHAPTER IV
# 1940-1960

In 1939, there was no reason to suppose that fashion would go into hiding. United States involvement in the war took us all by surprise, but its reality forced much of the fashion industry to sit it out. So many people can remember the 40's, they lived through those years and many have told me that reading about fashion is not like living with fashion. The average person wore what was appropriate, what had been dictated by some designer and made available.

In general the rather static state of fashion in the early 1940's stemmed from uncertainty and a sense of the fitness of things, drastic changes would have seemed unpatriotic. "From now until the war is won, we won't have radical changes in fashion" was the fashion decree.

Waste of anything, including material, was to be avoided, and the Government asked the designers not to use unnecessary lengths of fabric, not to make extreme changes, not to use excessive trimmings, in short, let the silhouette alone. One of the results of this dictum was cuffless slacks, and patterns of that date proudly stated the limited material it would take to make such and such a garment.

The lack of new directions for clothes did not quench the everlasting feminine search for chic. John Whitcomb, the talented illustrator (whose work is now being collected) delineated the 40's female in the idealized way the Gibson Girl spoke for the nineties. In time this fascinating female he depicted will become the nostalgia buff's pin-up.

It was a time when evening wear was seductive, and day wear had a neat simplicity. The dirndl skirt went well with a shirtwaist top, and the jacketed suit dress could go anywhere comfortably. Necklines were varied, choices were many, but the plunging neckline was a favorite.

Joan Crawford's squared shoulders speak for the time. This padded, wide shoulder was typical, but there were dresses with soft folds which fell gracefully, the black dress might have white lace edging on the revers and short sleeves, and the 'dickey' was considered a "high spot" of many frocks. It was worn under the dress so it presented a collar on a collar usually in contrasting colors. Anybody who ever owned or wore a 'dickey' can tell you it was one of the handiest things ever designed.

"The suit dress is the civilian's uniform for summer," said a popular magazine. It could be severely tailored or made in softer materials and draped, but the shoulders were padded and square. Saddle stitching was part of many dresses and the princess line was evident in the early 40's. The shirtwaist dress was given a new twist – "something different in the 'shirtfrock' " were the suspender like tucks, with the curved pockets following the line of the saddle stitching. There were luscious colors in dresses and dress suits, and there were still some prints.

As with most coats, there seem to be few collectors. The boxy coat of the 40's was padded at the shoulders and could be had in almost any length from waist to hem. The classic town coat was sometimes called a 'reefer' and was a fitted and flattering style. The technique of using long, narrow panels to make it slenderized the figure. There are many still around, and being rapidly pulled out of closets.

It may very well be the square shoulders that attracts, but whatever the reason it is toward the 40's that today's younger collectors are aiming. From the vantage point of those who wore them some of the exaggerated styles of the 40's do not seem that long ago, to those who were born in the 1960's they have such a different look as to be almost 'camp'.

Everywhere the vintage clothing stores are catering to this younger trade, some of whom are buying to wear, some to collect. The early 40's costumes were military oriented – in feminine attire this was reflected in the wide-shouldered, nipped-in waist look.

In men's clothing gabardine and khaki were being worn and colors were rather muted in keeping with the times. The military uniforms were seen everywhere, and now they are a big segment of clothing collecting. There are military shops devoted to the sale of these as well as anything connected with any of our branches of service. A lighter touch during this period was the porkpie hat, which was well liked for its flat crown and snap brim. It proved to be an enduring fashion.

Slacks, which had become necessary in the factories, were gaining favor, but slowly. It was a time of Rosie the Riveter and as she riveted, she needed suitable clothing. Although, we in the United States, are hard put to remember the pre-jeans era, this was it. When slacks did start to become part of the wardrobe, they were utilitarian and comfortable. They were, in fact, a bit on the baggy side, but they opened the way for the jeans revolution. In 1949 there were 'dungarees' or 'western style pants.' No one could ever have foreseen the effect these pants would have on future fashion. If they had, probably every design house would have dropped everything and geared up for production. Now we have high fashion jeans and poor Levi Strauss must be twirling in his grave at the sexy image.

It was the young Christian Dior who created consternation with his New Look in 1947. It was introduced in Paris and was not an immediate sensation. It was distinctly feminine in feeling, a rounded look, and Dior dropped the hemline with a thud heard round the world. The shoulder was rounded and the small waistline emphasized. The fashion permeated every segment of society and the tiny flowered hats sporting veils, or the veils on frames, are now eagerly sought after. They are very flattering, are well made, and many have survived. Hat collectors adore them, they take less space than older hats and come in a wide variety. They can still be worn with confidence, since they coordinate well with almost any costume, and are still inexpensive.

This was the time of matching the color of the gloves with the outfit, and if ever there is an underrated collecting field it is gloves. Fortunately the gloves of the 40's seem to have spurred many young people to buy them and care for them and I know of several good collections. It's amazing how few collectors look for them. They are often in beautiful shades of colors, and may have embroidery, or have the hand-tied French knots. The soft kid gloves of the 40's are especially fine, but prices on these have made substantial gains, possibly because people are impressed with the 'Made in France' label many of them carry. The gauntlet type have a distinctive look and the wrist length, or the long evening gloves with the little pearl buttons have often sold to those interested in jewelry or buttons. I wonder how many gloves have been sacrificed this way?

The dedicated clothing collector should keep in mind that while the great designers were providing fashion to the wealthy, America's off-the-rack capability was the finest in the world. Indeed it was not until the very late 1950's that Europe tried this way of merchandising, so most of the clothing available to us was probably bought off-the-rack and does not bear the great designer labels. If one were to find dresses with a Hattie Carnagie or Adrian label it would be a tremendous acquisition, but excellent copies, or New York's 7th Avenue originals are what we are most apt to add to our collections. Haute Couture boasts intricate and clever tailoring which flatters the figure and thus can command astronomical prices, but surely part of the price is paying for the label. Still, Paris was calling the tune.

When Dior decreed skirts should rise only 12 or 15 inches off the ground, women everywhere responded and discarded whole wardrobes in order to conform. The new dress code required high heels so the shoe image changed from the clunky, somewhat awkward footwear of the earlier 40's to the slimmer heel. This is an interesting period in shoes, the toes being rounded but blunted. It is difficult to visualize a collection of shoes, but having viewed one properly set out, is to become a convert.

The really wonderful aspect of Dior and his 'New Look' is that we do not have to wade through transitional clothing, the whole world knows, almost precisely to the minute, when Dior announced his new style. This circumstance is unique to clothing collectors and we should be properly grateful. We also know exactly when the fashion ended, by 1949 the style was phasing out and hemlines rose and the silhouette became less flaring. We who collect, or deal in clothing, can thank Dior for making the 1940's so exciting for us.

Seeking the couturier clothing involves some canny planning. Often the best source is the thrift shops maintained by women's auxiliaries whose members claim some social standing. If their social life is busy and requires much formal wear, they will often donate their outdated wardrobes to the thrift shops to which they volunteer. Recently, such a shop, a tiny one, in Westchester County, New York, boasted dresses by Norell and Mary Quant, and labels such as Saks 5th Avenue, Marshall Field and Lilli Ann. These were all day dresses, all of 40's and 50's vintage, and all together would have cost less than $50. Each of them a great addition to any collection.

The truth is that superior tailoring does not easily become dated, and often you will find women wearing couturier clothing made years ago. It is largely a revolutionary style, such as the 'New Look' which demands an entirely new wardrobe to keep in fashion. Nowadays we tend to ignore such a dictim from the arbiters of fashion and independence in dress is following independence in action.

So it is wise to track down shops run by organizations such as the Junior League, famous hospital auxiliaries and annual benefit auctions and sales put on by groups of socialites to benefit some worthy cause. These annual affairs, which sometimes benefit museums and branches of the arts, are probably some of the more serious places to shop for vintage, high-fashion clothing.

To do this, the collector has to read the newspapers diligently to keep aware of the upcoming sales. Some organizations will put you on their mailing list for occasions of this kind and if it is possible, request this. Usually clothing at these sales cost very little, since they are essentially high class rummage sales, and you will no doubt find many good buys. It does take time and effort but this can be rewarding.

Resale Shops are often the source of good finds, but tend to be more expensive since they must buy and clean clothing and do any repairing, and must also maintain a good looking shop in order to attract customers.

Goodwill, Salvation Army and St. Vincent de Paul were once treasure troves of older clothing, but their donations are off and competition among collectors who frequent these places is much keener. There are many people who know the exact time of donated merchandise deliveries and manage in that way to secure the goodies. Recently, though, a local St. Vincent de Paul had a remarkable collection of vintage shoes with buckles and bows which were being sold for $5 each pair, and were intended for wear with costumes on Halloween. Goodwill saves some of its better donated vintage clothing for its annual fashion show put on by the Goodwill Bags, but take a look if you're passing, because vintage clothing, like any other antique, is where you find it. But in this field today, you certainly have to keep looking.

Shoe collectors have a more difficult task since shoes have often been discarded as wear and tear make them less acceptable to good dress. There are rising numbers of people who are looking for vintage shoes. Reduced availability and sometimes less than perfect condition makes the search for old shoes discouraging to the faint hearted. The find, though, is well worth the hunt. Shoes of the 1940's are wholly unique. They can be clumsy looking and in no way resemble the footwear of the 1920's or earlier periods. Studious collectors should note that footwear can be categorized by the way the sole is attached to the upper.

American Footwear Industry lists 'cemented' when the sole and heel are attached by adhesion; 'molded' when the sole and heel are formed and the attachment to the upper is accomplished within a mold; 'sewn' is when the sole is attached to the upper by a stitched seam. The old method of nailing sole to upper was considered obsolete, which is a good time judgment for collectors.

Shoe styles have evolved and changed, often quite drastically, and are among the very typical artifacts of a given era. The wedgies of the 40's, the fairly narrow open toes, the tie oxford, are all characteristic.
times recently I have used a heavy leather shoulder bag from the 50's. It is finely made and has a heavy gilt closure.

The bulky look shoe complemented the dirndl dress and the military looking suit was perfect with the oxford. The 'peep toes' were the dress shoe of the day. As a 'go with' to shoe collecting the old wooden shoe forms are ideal. In this area though you compete with the antique collector and the interior decorator, take heart, they can't be everywhere.

With the end of World War II came a lighter look, and the mink stole was worn everywhere except the supermarket. The ubiquitous mink stole of that period has not made the comeback that other vintage furs, such as the silver fox jacket and neckpiece have achieved, but considering the small prices at which these stoles are marked, they are an excellent investment.

The 40's from beginning to end were a special time in America. The red, white and blue color scheme was used in clothing, there were ration cards, nylon hose, when available, was a cause of long lines, the hats are collectible but when worn today are not tilted over the eyebrow as was de rigeur in the 40's, but at a more flattering angle further back on the head.

The 40's was turban time. A classic fashion which has appeared and reappeared in some form, the turban was in part an answer to the demands of safety, to keep hair out of machinery at which women now worked in numbers. They affected snoods and hair nets and they started the passion for pants.

As the 1940's began, fashion direction was uncertain, but people in general were becoming much more casual about dress. This decade really marked the beginning of informality and complete independence from rigid fashion demands.

As the decade ended it bacame memorable for synthetic fibers, the boxy, square shoulders and the return of the female figure, for boleros and the "New Look". For clothing collectors the indicators of 40's fashions are the smaller hat, the square, padded shoulders, narrow waist. The strapless evening gown, supposedly held up by a prayer, was almost standard. The military influence lent itself to the Eisenhower jacket both for men and women, and pea coats and khaki sportswear remained popular for men.

The years 1940 to 1950 are one of the strongest in the clothing collecting field. Several years ago it began to attract young people, both male and female, and the trend continues. No wonder, it seems to have everything a good collection demands, unique styling, short skirts, long skirts, strapless gowns, luxurious furs, coats of many designs, unusual shoes, and lovely handbags. There is very little the collector cannot find from the 40's, to fit his purse and preference. Close your eyes, make a clothing wish, then check out the 1940's.

As the country moved into a new decade we seemed to be searching for security. Conservatism was the new creed. This is especially reflected in the menswear of the early 1950's when the trim, quiet look was in vogue. This was a distinct change from the late 1940's brighter colors. Now dark shades of blue and brown and gray took over the scene. In 1953 the gray flannel suit began its reign.

President Eisenhower refused to bow to tradition at his inauguration in 1953 when he chose to wear a jacket with his striped trousers and a homburg instead of the usual top hat and cutaway. Looking back on his decision, it seems merely the choice of a man who wanted more informality, a less rigid way of dealing with ordinary affairs. In reality, it was a ripple on the surface of what was to become almost a full scale revolt by the young. It was a forerunner of entirely new directions both in clothing and lifestyle, and Elvis Presley was waiting in the wings with his Levis and suede shoes.

The second World War emancipated everyone, and fashion was on the way to becoming anything anyone wanted it to be. If the early 50's had any typical characteristics it was probably the normal waistline, narrow slim skirts at midcalf which were soon to shorten again. The A line which Dior ordained in 1958 had a very wide skirt draped from sloping shoulders, and the skirt just below the knee. As the 50's progressed so did the skirt, upward.

This was generally a period of transition when almost anything was acceptable. Some of the full skirts of the 40's persisted into the early fifties. The long fitted bodice of 1954 and 1955 emphasized a beautiful figure. The focus was on the neckline and hipline, and dresses were usually worn with the pointed shoe with high slender heels. Heels on the shoes became even higher before the end of the decade. They were considered a menace and were decried by promoters of good posture.

The bustline was accentuated, the waistline was high, and the strapless evening gown was still being worn by the end of 1958. Knitwear, especially the Chanel style jacketed dress and suit became classic and went easily from office to cocktails. The pillbox hat was sitting pertly on most female heads, but with the modified cloche hats, organza veilings, very tiny hats, wide brimmed hats, headbands, small feather confections, the hat collector can have a field day with the 50's.

Recently, while I was browsing in a small vintage clothing shop, an elderly lady approached me in a state of high excitement. "Look at this," she exclaimed, holding up a rather nondescript gray straw hat, "this is a Dior, look at the label." I did. It surely was a Dior, if rather faded, and since she explained she was a hat collector I could understand her exuberance. The label itself was large and striking, it was a vintange hat, and the price was not very high, and no doubt she felt she had a bargain. I would have recommended perhaps, a hat bearing no label, which sat on a nearby stand and was of the same vintage — a small, crescent shape with a mesh veil, flowers on the crown and a velvet ribbon flat bow, an enticing affair and costing just a bit less. There was that label, though, and we collectors have to make our choices. Vintage clothing bearing designer labels will usually cost more. "Snob appeal", one dealer says.

This is not true for shoe collectors, the label does not make the shoe, except for a few outstanding makers and the mark of an exclusive shoe store. Most dealers price according to condition and era. Collectors who buy also to wear are concerned with fit, and this is a frustrating situation. The 50's shoes are fairly easy to find, although here again, their appeal to younger collectors causes the fine examples to sell quickly. These very high, slender heels are more difficult to find, the styles without sides or cut deeply on the sides are very flattering to the foot, but the smallish, open toes are the big goal. The alligator and lizard skin shoes and handbags of this era are intrinsically valuable but condition should be good. Many closets still harbor shoes of this period.

Budget conscious collectors should visit their thrift shops more often. In a recent tour I found large numbers of the 50's coats. These were unusually attractive, especially in the late 50's. Dior (the man did everything) had introduced his A line with its wide hemline and narrow shoulders and these are found frequently. The tie neckline also is a very pretty style. There are also the very typical three quarter length coats and the shortie coats with the belt in the back. Another attractive coat from that period has the shawl collar and narrow hem which is often furred. People who buy and wear these coats profess to admire their 'old fashioned' look. People who buy then as a collectible have found a veritable gold mine.

The sheath was the big news in the 50's and in keeping with the times it was an easy and comfortable style. Women were seen everywhere in the narrow but unconfining dress. Capri pants and the skirts — circle skirts, were wide and often stiffened. The total ensemble was usually skirt and blouse or capri pants, or skirt with sweater or blouse. Handbags were casual and that was the attraction of the shoulder bag.

Handbags are a joy to collect. Not as pretty as the beaded bags or as intricately worked as the tapestries, not as spectacular as the best of the art deco, the 50's handbags have a special place. They often have unusual handles of metal, leather or plastic. Reptile skin was commonly used and some women were still carrying the corde.

As always with pocketbooks or purses, shapes are quite varied, and it is often the handles that lend interest. It is almost a cliche to say that fashion comes full circle every generation, but there is ample proof that this is true. Several times recently I have used a heavy leather shoulder bag from the 50's. It is finely made and has a heavy gilt closure. It is large enough to hold all the necessities and it still strikes a fashion note. There is a timelessness about some things and good leather, simply worked, is one. Except for the wide, braided shoulder strap which was used frequently on bags of this type in the 50's, only the most sophisticated fashion critic could date the bag.

Gifts for the men in the years of the early 50's included a Shaefer "snorkel fountain pen", which would be a great find; or a yellow and black striped Italian denim butler's jacket, which would be useful if you wanted to impress guests; and waterproof deerskin slippers with foam rubber lining, at $12.50 a pair.

Ski parkas were being touted in bright colors and 'warmly lined for warmth'.

Clear plastic umbrellas cheered the rainy days, and a wool jersey scarf lined in hand printed silk was the offering from 'Vera'. Today a complete and very thorough collection of scarves by 'Vera' could easily be made, they seem to turn up everywhere.

Mother and Daughter dresses were popular. A charming collection this would be — the adult's dress and the matching childs's dress displayed side by side. Almost like collecting in pairs, the large and the miniature. To date,

193

I have found only two such pairs and they are in a private collection. Should a person happen on a set and the dealer would be foolish enough to break it up, don't hesitate, buy both. Not only were they eye-catching in their day, and interesting to us today, but think of the future and how unusual the matching pieces will be.

Hats of both mother and daughter often matched too, but is is almost too much to expect that four such articles will be found intact. Still, it's intriguing and cries out for a determined collector. Someone with an eye for the unusual. It is these fads which sustain popularity for awhile and then disappear which sometimes become the basis for the most valuable collections.

Plisse was an oft-heard name in the early 50's, but we don't hear it too much anymore. It is cotton, with a crinkle effect and usually patterned. It was 'easy iron' and was widely used in nightwear and some of the nightgowns from which it was made, are attractive enough to be worn for summer evening wear. Many plisse garments are striped or have small prints and almost all are very pretty. When some young collector decides this is the case, you may see a brightly colored plisse printed nightgown of the 1950's doing double duty.

With the variety of fabrics available in the 1950's, it is probably safe to say that lingerie could be made of almost any material. It is also safe to say that it was exceedingly lovely for the most part. The shortie nightie which ended just below the knee sometimes had tiny sleeves or cape effects and touches of lace and ribbon which made for a dainty, delightful morsel. The colors, petal pink, or heaven blue, or even buttercup are delectable. Longer gowns were also worn, many of them made of nylon tricot which boasted the same 'easy care'. Nylon is a high-strength, resilient synthetic, so many survive today. This is a great time to collect these pretty things including the full underslips and the handy half slips which have wide lace trim.

Barbizon was the big name in lingerie if you are label conscious, but there were many manufacturers producing beautiful underwear. Some of the fancy slips are made in the gored fashion which prevented bunching at the waist. They were expertly tailored and make a wonderful collection. It was one of the best of times for women's undergarments and before these get away from us we should make every effort to include them in our collections. They require little care and make a colorful display.

The undergarments fitted well under the clothing. One of the most delightful of fashions in the 50's was the two piece suit, jacket and skirt, in rayon gabardine. The jacket was short, with a flare and a Peter Pan collar with double rows of buttons, the skirt was straight and fairly narrow. It was one of those outfits which went everywhere, and I have seen several similar outfits lately, so it must have been a big seller. It was practical, maybe that's why. Women were losing their zest for using a different garment for every occasion and a dress that went through the day was a plus. With this two piece suit the whole look could be changed with a new sweater or blouse and with the jacket left open.

Dolman sleeves were still being worn in the 50's and the loose, and longish sweater often had them. The Dolman sleeve is one of the most comfortable ever devised, so it's easy to see that we have moved even deeper into our desire for ease and practicality in clothes.

The Italian fashion collections became very important and without doubt they had a flair for color and design which began to take the lead in certain directions. They introduced innovative ski wear and magnificent shoe style. It wasn't the Italians, though, who created a sensation in the tennis world. It was Ted Tinling who dressed Gussie Moran in lace trimmed panties which caused a furor. She played at Wimbledon in 1949, and those panties banished forever the image of the staid and proper tennis buff.

A small development really, that Moran outfit, completely modest by today's standards, but it led to a new fashion standard for tennis players and more enjoyment for fans. One reporter maintained that people were going to watch tennis when Gussie played only to see what she would wear.

Tennis gear is collectible on all levels, the tennis wear itself is an excellent collectible because it did not change much until 1949. Since that time it has become as varied as one could want. The dresses were usually white, one piece and belted and pleated. By the 40's the one piece dress was shorter, and soon the outfit became two pieces. Tennis dresses are distinctive and to a sportsminded person would present an exciting challenge. I do not know anyone with such a collection so it has a relatively open future. As with anything that has not yet really caught on, prices should be minimal.

Many things from the 50's are ideal collectibles. The eyeglasses are strictly for fun and profit. Rhinestones or brilliants were set into plastic frames which were called 'harlequin' and looked like a giant butterfly. Until about a year ago, these could be bought for a dollar or two anywhere, now they are commanding prices of $25-65 depending on their amount of decoration and how bizarre they are. Women are wearing them and there is a trend to buy a pair and replace the lenses with your own prescription. They are certainly conversation pieces. These wild spectacles did not much influence men's eye wear, they were still sporting the horn rims.

There is much to commend the 1950's as a collecting field, but for many it is still too close.

Designers appreciate it and many adaptations of the 40's and 50's styles are evident in the new clothing.

The 1950's are a closed chapter which many of us remember vividly, and that makes it easy to dismiss the 50's as yet too recent to be considered vintage fashion. The collecting world has become so competitive and unpredictable that it is almost dangerous to discard anything made yesterday.

On that note, the 1950's seem akin to the dinosaur age. Much of the clothing has not yet come out of the closet, and thrifty women everywhere have saved a quantity of it, now hanging neatly all in a row and never worn. Yet they cannot part with it.

When more of it comes into the marketplace, potential collectors will be surprised at its beauty, its charm or its whimsy, depending on the mood.

Collecting is largely a point of view. From the vantage point of 1987, it may be difficult to keep the 1950's in perspective. Try — the fashions of those years may bring big rewards.

## 1960

A peek into the 1960's should send collectors scurrying about to try to amass a collection of that decade's most controversial style — the mini skirt. It looked great on young, long-stemmed American beauties, on all others it was an abomination.

Mary Quant evoked it, and has been quoted as saying that she felt at the time that the 1960's needed "a revolution" and frankly admits that it was intended as a fashion for the young. In fact, it seems to have been an acknowledgement that young people were a major market, they had plenty of money to spend and were more than willing to spend it.

There were other styles and other happenings during the following years, there are other clothes and other accessories to search for, but at this time, before they disappear, the collector should be alert to the mini.

Fifty years from now the uninitiated are going to look at all those minis and think, Gosh, people were short in the 1960's.

Everyday or house dress of 1942. Printed percale coat frock, modified torso style with white binding trim on yoke and pockets, square padded shoulders. Value $35-50.

Two piece jacket dress, self cuffs, raglan sleeves, sateen. C. 1944. Value $125-145.

1940s white organdy, with red dots, three tiers, red binding trim. Red belt. Value $65-85.

Left: Tan flannel dress with asymetrical button closing on waist. Tucks, collarless, square padded shoulders, bracelet length sleeves. Shoes are the well remembered loafers. Dress $45-55.

Center: Another three piece suit. The suit is blue and white check, matching coat of solid blue. Nipped in waist and wide shoulders distinguish the suit, the coat has a boxy look. Value of 3 pieces $135-150.

Right: Purple crepe dress with square neckline, padded shoulders, elongated tucks at waistline, belted in self material. Worn with black wrist length gloves and the hat with the popular front large standing bow with veil which is so typical of the period. The pageboy hairdo was well suited to these hats. Value of dress $50-55.

Another deceptively simple looking dress of the 40s. It is black crepe and black taffeta with a large bow at the neckline. Long waisted and mid calf length it molds the figure in a provocative way. 3/4 length sleeve. Although this dress bears no label it was bought in Lord & Taylor's, New York. Worn in 1942 with black suede pumps. Value of dress $200-250.

This beautifully crafted tissue-taffeta blue-green dress of the 1940s displays all the qualities which are making the clothing of this era so collectible. The zippered front closing is carefully hidden beneath the fly which lies perfectly flat, the Peter Pan collar is covered with small white beads, the waistline is long and fitted to the hips and over all while this dress would seem to have a distinctly demure look, it is in fact quite seductive on the right figure. Mid calf length. Value $200-250.

1950s dark brown faille dress with self cabbage roses on shoulders. Cap sleeves, belted. Skirt falls just below knee. The attention to detail in 'off the rack' clothing of the 40s and 50s is often meticulous and to today's new collectors rather unexpected. Value of dress $150-175. The brown lizard shoes have very high heels.

Turquoise faille, empire style, full skirted dress of the 40s. Plastic buttons, V neck. Ann Fogarty label. Value $125-175. The greenish-blue enamel necklace of the 1930s blends perfectly with the dress.

Two piece outfit from the 1940's. Quilted blue midi length skirt worn with Lilli Ann of San Francisco jacket, dark blue textured wool accented with white bead work on collar and on the wide cuffed sleeves. Skirt, value $45-70. Jacket, value $45-65. Model is wearing a snood.

A classic Chanel type suit of brown tweed with brown caracul fur collar which runs down to waist. 1950s. Still wearable and in perfect taste for almost any but the most formal occasion. Value $175-200.

In 1948 dresses were longer, fur pieces were still very much in evidence, veils and the same high front decorations were visible on the hats, gauntlet gloves were popular and the suit continued fashionable. Wool with gabardine, beautifully tailored, simple lines, nipped-in waist, small double collar, straight skirt. Value of this wonderful suit, $200-250.

The silhouette of 1949. Two piece dress, double breasted with large self-covered buttons, gauntlet cuffs, wide revers and standing collar. Very wide, circular skirt. Gorgeous and eminently flattering to the wearer. Silk and worsted combination. Value $185-210.

A two-piece taffeta dress with short jacket and back bow interest. Full skirt, thoroughly typical of dresses of 1949. Value $100-125.

1946. These contrasting skirt and blouse outfits were sometimes referred to as 'plaid and plain'. Cotton and rayon-linen, they were cool and easy to keep for summer. Value $45-55.

The fleecy wool short coat was a style that went over everything and could be worn for years and years. Women who wore these in the 1940's and still own them can be seen wearing them on a given summer evening. White. Value $65-75.

Another jacket dress of 1949. Wool and worsted suit in hunting green. This is 2 piece with the jacket covering a collarless dress. Value $125-145.

One of the biggest fashion notes of the 1940's was the ladies' three piece suit, the coat matched the suit or was in a contrasting color. This navy blue 3-piecer has the 3/4 length coat which is a very flattering coat length on some figures. Wool, the suit is collarless. Value of 3 pieces $150-175.

A 'little' wool dress of 1949, splinter pleated skirt, top buttons to neck and has standing collar with 3/4 length sleeves. Dashing. Charm bracelets were in vogue and the dress has a rhinestone and gilt pin. Value of dress $185-210.

1964 Mini skirt dress in cotton. Value $45-55. Photo courtesy of Butterick Archives

Party dress of 1960's. Dotted organdy embroidered with satin ribbon inserts. Short gloves. Value of dress is $35-45. This is the time to be seeking the clothing of the early 1960's.

1965. Dress of houndstooth check with white pique flat collar and cuffs on long, rather loose sleeves. Knee length. Very high band of contrasting color maintains the straight line of the garment since it takes the eye away from the waistline. Value $45-55. Courtesy of Butterick Archives.

Late 1960's one piece dress which resembles a two piece outfit. Polyester and cotton. Value $30-35. Clothing of the 60's is not yet a genuine collector's item. Courtesy Butterick Archives.

1944. Blue wool coat, fitted, white fox collar, $250-285. Brown felt envelope handbag, satin lined, brass engraved triangle on flap, $85-95. Brown brimmed felt cloche hat, $45-55. (WW II) military uniform, jacket with decorations, $100-110. Complete uniform, $135-165.

1968 - Knitwear full length coat. $50-55. Courtesy Butterick Archives.

The collarless rather elegant coat of the early 1960's in polyester and cotton. Short; large pockets. Value $55-65.

The still popular silver fox jacket, c. 1941. Value, $650-750. Black satin evening dress, c. 1935. Value $195-220. Satin shoes, worn originally with the dress shown, buckles are part of shoe itself, $75-100.

1940's dress. Black crepe with peplum and sleeves trimmed in sequins. Accessories include black cotton cut-worked embroidered gloves, sequined hat with feather, snood and a stole of four stone martins. Values: dress, $110-120; fur piece, $200-225; gloves, $15-20; hat, $20-35.

1940's dress of brown crepe with beige flowers, low waistline drape ends on left side. Mid calf length. Value $85-$125. Worn with beige and bone kid shoes which have an ankle strap. Beige straw hat with wide brim by Mr. John. Value of hat $35-50. Stone marten fur scarf $250-275.

Full length wool coat with classic white fox collar; brown with bands of contrasting darker brown. C. 1950. Value $750-850.

Black crepe mid-calf length dress, V-neck, belted. C. 1949, black satin shoes with self bows, original to the costume. Double strand pearl choker, pink. Values: dress, $125-135; shoes, $60-80.

Cocktail dress, 1945. Black crepe top, V-off the shoulder neck, ruffled tiers of black net over taffeta skirt. Net and embroidered see-through shoes. Value, dress, $135-175; shoes, $45-65.

1950. Light pink strapless taffeta evening gown with large bow accenting one shoulder. Full skirt lined with a stiffened attached slip. Value, $125-175.

Below: Mainbocher short evening dress, c. 1955 of black broderie anglaise over black net, with boat neckline, fitted bodice and full skirt, appliqued up the center with a black satin band curving to form a second shoulder strap on the left with black cotton and net slip. Label: Mainbocher, Inc. The value of this dress should be in the $300-400 range but the dress brought less at the recent Ruth Gordon auction at Doyle Galleries in New York. This is what motivates collectors, the bargains which consistently occur in this still undercollected field. Pre-auction estimate of this dress was $200-300. The 1950's really fine garments are just beginning to come into their own.

Above: Blue cotton lace with attached taffeta underslip. Cocktail or 'Mother-of-the-Bride' dress. 1952. Tasteful, small rhinestone patterns on collar. Value, $150-160. Blue gray kid shoes, worn with dress originally. Value $40-50.

A spectacular formal cocktail dress from Frederick's of Hollywood, 1958-1959. Silver lame with wide black taffeta ruffle on skirt, large black taffeta rose on left side above hemline. Value $175-250.

Above: Mainbocher cocktail dress, 1960's of deep blue velvet-cut-to-satin, the sleeveless dress with a slightly gathered skirt, no label. Value $150-200. The future of dresses of this quality is unlimited.

Above: Chanel cocktail dress, late 1950's, early 1960s, of minutely tucked black chiffon with bootlace straps and fitted midriff of black satin, skirt stiffened with horsehair at the hem to flare out in a pleated ruffle. Label: Chanel $450-600.

Mainbocher evening dress, c. 1955. Pale mint green silk chiffon over aquamarine tulle, with halter bodice and full skirt, the bodice trimmed with ball-edged satin ribbon in pink over yellow and with an ornament pin of green and turquoise jewels. Label 'Mainbocher, Inc.' Value $250-300.

The back interest of the 1930's (which has never entirely gone out of style) continued to some degree into the 40's. In 1945 this sophisticated lady was wearing black with halter neck and low cut back accentuated with a large satin ribbon bow at the waist. The dress is fully draped in the back, rather straight in front. A stunning garment. Value in silk chiffon $400-500. Worn with long kid gloves.

Strapless gown of 1952. These are now in the category fast approaching the beaded dresses of the 1920's. Although almost every prom saw a profusion of these in the 40's and early 50's many must still be in the closet. Much depends on the material, tailoring, trim and general effect but the more extravagant such as this commands $200-250. Every collector should be alert to the strapless evening gown that dominated evening fashions for so long.

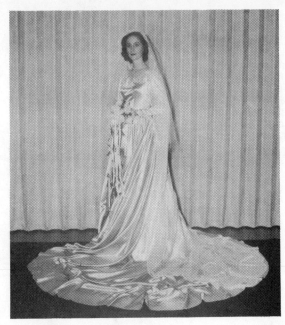

Formal wedding gown, 1951. Candlelight satin, appliqued leaves and seed pearls at neck. Train. Saks 5th Ave. Value $800-1000.

Lingerie, 1940. Nightgown and bedjacket of rayon crepe in a floral pattern. Maize and white. Original Bennington label, a manufacturer of fine lingerie. Value of set, $85-125. These have been known to be worn as formals.

A rayon nightgown with lacey bodice, bare midriff and lace 'cocktail' bottom. Value $45-55. 1948 name of this fashion was "Diversion".

Mother and Daughter play outfits of 1946. These could be worn for sunning, or at the beach, to play in, even as pajamas. Sanforized combed cotton, small prints of kittens. Pink. Adult size $35-45. Child's size either one piece or two pieces $30-35.

Pajamas with matching scuffs of 1949. Cotton broadcloth, coat could be used as a 'brunchie', striped trim on collar and pockets. Scuffs have same trim. Set $45-50 in excellent condition.

Lingerie. Pink pleated nylon nightgown, usually referred to as "Marilyn Monroe" nightwear; turquoise short slip with attached garters, spandex, pleated; value of these is $35-45 each; ivory satin nightgown bias cut, pink embroidered rosebuds on bodice. Long length value $35-45.

Taffeta housecoat of fine houndstooth check with embroidered collar and pockets. Self belting, jet buttons, 3/4 sleeves. Late 1940s. $95-145.

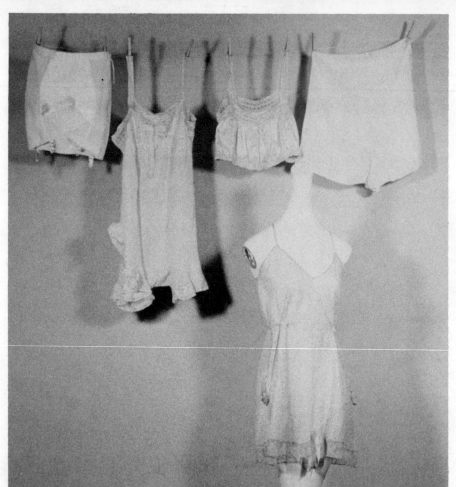

Lingerie. Stretch girdle, 1940s, unworn, attached garters. In 'as new' condition these are a worthwhile addition to a collection and as yet no real surge is on to find them. Value $10-20; silk crepe teddy, 1920s, $85-120. 1920s silk bandeau $45-65, 1940s rayon crepe panties with hand crocheted ornament, value in unworn condition $15-20; gorgeous teddy of silk and lace with satin ribbons. $100-145.

1940. Pretty and efficient, the apron should not be underestimated as a clothing collectible. Cotton. In good condition, $5-15.

A fancier apron of 1942. Woven dotted swiss in pastel blue. Smocking in deep bands at the waist and pockets. Original cost $1.50. Value $5-15.

Playclothes in 1942-43. Full flared shorts with belt, worn with striped cotton top. Set $20-25.

A maternity bathing suit of the 1950s, blue cotton with blue and white printed scarf belt. Expansion elastic under front panel. $10-20. Somewhat unusual.

1940s skirted bathing suit. White with green print. Jersey. $15-25, old 'Kleinert' bathing cap. $5-10.

A rather modest bathing suit of the early 1960's, two-piece, polyester. Value $5-15.

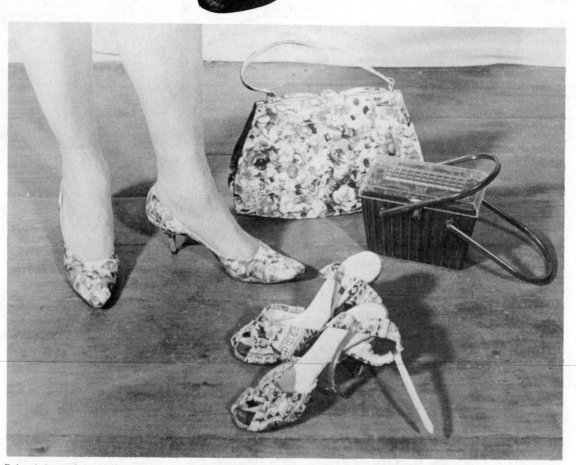

The shoes of the 1940's are quite distinctive. Toeless and sling back vied with the rounded toe pump. All of these are suede. Value $25-35.

A high heeled, platform shoe of 1948. Black suede trimmed with black satin. Value $30-35.

In 1949 "wedges or wedgies" were the rage. They were advertised as "dramatizing your proportions with the perfect height" although many people considered them ugly. An interesting fashion note nonetheless. Value $35-40.

Pointed shoes of the 1960s, printed with multi-colored silk, 2½" heel, $30-35; matching handbag $25-35; Ankle strap printed sandals of the 1940s, 3" heel, $35-50.

Accessories: alligator shoes, sharply pointed toe, 1957. Value $75-100. Corde handbag, plastic handle, 1942. Value, $30-35. Alligator handbag, 1952. Value $100-135.

The shoe toe in 1959 was almost a stiletto. Kid with buckle trim and spike heels. Value of these is soaring. $35-40.

Accessories of 1940-1960. Gloves of various lengths and adornment from this period are remarkably well made and ornamented. They are still very easy to find, quite inexpensive and make a pretty, rather fascinating collectible. Values vary depending on length, material and trim but the long kid gloves with small pearl buttons, the nylon and the crochet are all moving up in price. Starting price is about $3-5 on ordinary types of cotton, $10-15 on others. Now is definitely the time to start searching for the unusually colored, decorated cotton gloves.

Shoes: Black silk with faille bow knot, 1960's, value $15-25; black and white 'spectators'; leather silver sling pumps with open toe; brown leather tie; silver leather ankle strap; 60's print pump; alligator with bow; 1950's lizard pump; lucite with rhinestones embedded into the shoe as well as the entire heel. Shoes are also variable in price, generally begin around $20 for the ordinary types; $45 for the reptile and higher for the well-made rhinestone.

Handbags: left top is purple and clear lucite of the 1940's. These bags are becoming expensive, are often bizarre and are valued at a minimum $35-40. A brown and clear lucite of the 40's; crochet handbag on a yellow plastic frame which embodies the handle. Yellow plastic discs are attached to the crochet, 1950s, $15-20; handbag of crocheted raffia, plastic beads on a crochet base, plastic chain handle $15-20. These bags are charming with a unique look, quite colorful and still available. The bag on the right is late beaded red and white, blue, green on blue rayon. Plastic top and closure. $20-25.

The loafer persisted throughout the 40's. Leather with buckle. Value $20-25.

In 1987 it is hard to visualize the everyday use of gloves. There are now many collectors of the pretty, well made gloves of these years, but they are still underpriced for their quality and flair. Top, double woven cotton, lockstitch sewn, eyelet top. White. Value $5-15.

Center, sueded rayon, stitched welts. Value $15-20. Bottom, the nylon gloves which are being made again. Dainty eyelet embroidered cuffs. Value $10-15. One of the greatest attractions of these glove collections is the variety of lovely colors of the fabrics

The late 1940's tailored look called for plain shoes. The loafer, the oxford, and the staple pump. All of leather and well made. Value in excellent condtiion $25-35.

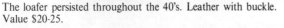

The little felt hat, a wardrobe staple. This is 'smooth-as-silk felt' with velvet trim and butterfly bow. 1949. Value $15-20.

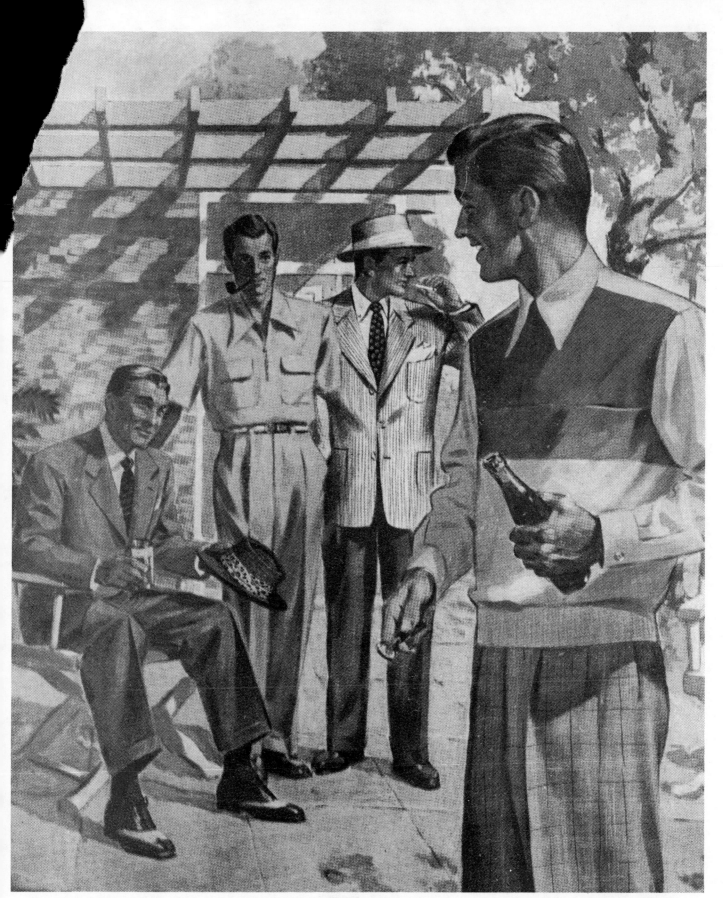

The whole trend in 50's men's clothing was toward the casual. Left, an all rayon gabardine suit worn with a coconut straw hat, suit $85-100; hat with printed band $5-15; denim shirt and slacks, set $35-45; cord sports jacket (rayon, nylon, cotton blend) $20-30; Glen plaid slacks $20-25; sports shirt in dual colors with long sleeves $20-25. Men's ties now fill a variety of functions – quilting, skirts, reconstructed as ladies' ties, belts, these older wide ties are a versatile hobby item. The silk material can be either subdued or quite wildly patterned to fit any taste. Value of each tie in silk $5-20; socks in pristine condition are almost impossible to find but if available are $5-10 especially in bold plaids.

The dandy of 1949. He wears a lightweight summer suit of tropical worsted with an unlined jacket. Snappy bow tie, pocket handkerchief and summer straw hat with wide brim. Wide shoulders on suit jacket. Value of suit $95-125. It is interesting that men's clothing of this period is as popular if not more so with collectors and potential wearers, than the female apparel.

Couple wearing the rather loose clothing of 1952. Men's trousers were wide and cuffed, jacket long, snap brim fedora; woman wears a full back 3/4 length coat over dark skirt, large fitted beret, stockings have defined heels and seams. Shoes have rounded toe. Clothing of this type still available and inexpensive. The open toe was prevalent in 1952 and shoes were not too much changed from previous years. Price ranges previously noted.

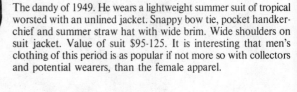

In the late 1940's men were fond of pin stripes. This is gray and white, has a neat, tailored look and has the usual tie and handkerchief combination. Value of this wool suit is $150-185.